Antony and Cleopatra

WILLIAM SHAKESPEARE

Guide written by
Stewart Martin

A Letts Literature Guide

First published 1995

Letts Educational
Aldine House
Aldine Place
London W12 8AW
0181 743 7514

Typeset by Jordan Publishing Design

Text design Jonathan Barnard

Cover and text illustrations Hugh Marshall

Graphic illustration Hugh Marshall

British Library Cataloguing in Publication Data
A CIP record for this book is available from the British Library

ISBN 1 85758 267 5

Printed and bound in Great Britain
by Ashford Colour Press Ltd,
Gosport, Hants.

Letts Educational is the trading name of BPP (Letts Educational) Ltd

Contents

Plot synopsis 4

Who's who in *Antony and Cleopatra* 8

Themes and images in *Antony and Cleopatra* 15

Text commentary Act One 18

Self-test questions Act One 23

Text commentary Act Two 24

Self-test questions Act Two 29

Text commentary Act Three 30

Self-test questions Act Three 39

Text commentary Act Four 40

Self-test questions Act Four 47

Text commentary Act Five 49

Self-test questions Act Five 54

Self-test answers 56

Writing an examination essay 64

Plot synopsis

The plot of *Antony and Cleopatra* follows on from the end of *Julius Caesar.* After the murder of Caesar and the defeat of the conspirators Brutus and Cassius, the Roman Empire is now run by three triumvirs (soldier administrators): Mark Antony, Octavius Caesar and Lepidus. The story is set in ancient Egypt, Italy and Greece, and as a traditional tale from classical literature, although Shakespeare significantly amended historical accounts.

Antony, who commands the eastern section of the empire, has been neglecting his responsibilities because of his passionate love affair with Cleopatra, Queen of Egypt. His soldiers are dispirited by their leader's behaviour and the rest of the Empire is suffering from internal rebellion: Sextus Pompeius is defying Caesar's authority; the Parthians have successfully invaded part of the Empire; and Antony's wife Fulvia and brother Lucius have unsuccessfully rebelled against Caesar in Italy, following which Fulvia has died on her way to see Antony. Because of these events, Antony decides he must leave Egypt and return to Rome. This response surprises Caesar, who holds a low opinion of Antony because of his behaviour.

At a rather frosty meeting of the triumvirs in Rome, Antony agrees that in order to keep their alliance together he will marry Caesar's sister, Octavia. The triumvirs decide to hold a meeting with the rebellious Pompey, at which they agree a peace treaty. Following a conversation with a soothsayer, who says the younger Caesar's fortunes will always outshine his, Antony decides to follow his heart and return to Egypt.

Whilst en route to Egypt with Octavia, Antony learns that Caesar has broken the peace treaty by renewing the war against Pompey, who is now defeated, and has then sentenced the other triumvir, Lepidus, to death. Antony realises that this now leaves the entire Empire controlled by himself and Caesar. Antony therefore sends his new wife Octavia to Rome to discuss events with Caesar, while he returns to Egypt and Cleopatra. This triggers hostilities between Caesar and Antony for control of the whole Empire.

In Egypt, Cleopatra joins forces with Antony, who holds a lavish public ceremony at which he enthrones Cleopatra and her children as monarchs of the Eastern Roman Empire. Back in Rome, news of this ceremony, together with Octavia's sudden arrival, enrages Caesar. Knowing it will lead to war, Caesar offers half of all his conquests if Antony does likewise.

The war begins in Actium, where Antony is defeated after he listens to Cleopatra. She says they should fight at sea, so Antony ignores Enobarbus and his generals, who all tell him to fight on land where his forces are strongest.

During the battle Cleopatra turns her ship and flees, followed by Antony. Caesar chases them to Alexandria, where Antony, furious with Cleopatra and so disgusted at losing the battle that he contemplates suicide, agrees to seek terms for peace after he and Cleopatra are reconciled. Caesar refuses this and says he will grant Cleopatra whatever she wishes if she will either banish Antony or kill him. Feeling insulted, Antony challenges Caesar to single combat, but this also is refused by Caesar, who sends a messenger to attempt to win over Cleopatra to his side. Antony charges Cleopatra with thinking of betraying him, an accusation which she denies.

Antony decides that he will fight Caesar in one desperate final battle, even though many of his allies and trusted servants, including Enobarbus, have by now deserted him. Antony is victorious in his land battle and celebrates that night, while Enobarbus, in Caesar's camp, dies of shame at his treachery. The following day Antony sees all his sea-forces surrender to Caesar and, realising that everything is now lost, fiercely accuses Cleopatra of betraying him. Cleopatra is so frightened at Antony's fury that she hides in her monument. This was Cleopatra's tomb, prepared for her eventual death, and would have been a large stone structure with more than one storey. In view of the play's ending, it is ironic that it is here that she hides and sends word to Antony that she has killed herself. This news so dispirits Antony, who is already considering suicide, that he orders his servant Eros to kill him, but Eros takes his own life rather than obey. Antony falls on his own sword, but manages only to give himself a mortal wound. Meanwhile, Cleopatra has become worried at the effect her message may have had on Antony and sends another messenger to tell him that she is in fact alive.

Antony is taken to Cleopatra and dies in her arms, after which she vows to follow him. Caesar and his followers are saddened when they hear of Antony's death, but Caesar sends messengers to prevent Cleopatra taking her own life, because he wishes to lead her in triumph in Rome. His soldiers gain secret entry to the monument and thwart Cleopatra's attempt to stab herself. Realising what Caesar is planning, Cleopatra buys time by negotiating with him, but arranges for poisonous asps to be smuggled in past his guards. She dresses in her royal robes and, using the asps, commits suicide. Caesar is impressed by her noble death and, accepting that the lovers have defeated him, orders that they be buried together and given a dignified state funeral.

Note: Different editions of a Shakespeare play are usually very similar, although they may show occasional variation in spelling, punctuation and the arrangement of the lines. You may even come across differences in act or scene divisions, but this should produce no difficulties for you in identifying the particular point or section being commented on in this Guide. The quotations and comments in this Guide are referenced to the Arden edition of the play.

ANTONY IS TORN BETWEEN THE MILITARY HONOUR AND FAMILIAL DUTY

OF ROME AND THE SENSUALITY AND LUXURIOUS LIFE-STYLE OF EGYPT

EGYPT

Who's who in *Antony and Cleopatra*

Antony

As the play opens, Antony is described in terms which contrast what he once was with what he has become. The brave general and great leader seen in *Julius Caesar,* who subsequently became widely respected as a pillar of military might and brave leadership in the Empire, is now a figure in decline, a man who has been tempted astray by the soft life and his passion for Cleopatra. Antony is therefore presented to the audience as a character set in a political, military and emotional context. But his emotions for Cleopatra do not wholly override his political and military intelligence; he returns to Rome and agrees to a tactical marriage to Caesar's sister, Octavia, as a way of sealing the peace treaty between the two men. He is also sometimes distrustful of Cleopatra and accuses her more than once of betraying him both emotionally and politically, and of causing his military defeats. It is only after Antony's death that the audience can be sure of Cleopatra's emotions for him, because until then her actions often seem at odds with her words. Antony is never sure of her – he dies assuming that Cleopatra will forge some kind of political alliance with Caesar.

Antony's search for absolute love and absolute power is frustrated on both counts. As the events of the play unfold he appears to be less and less in command of his life, his military fortunes and himself, yet is well thought of by his enemies. Those closest to him are prepared to give up their lives rather than harm him: even the cynical Enobarbus eventually dies of grief at having deserted so generous a man and Antony's servant Eros takes his own life rather than help to kill his master.

The soothsayer tells Antony that his days in the ascendant are over – Caesar's fortune will always outshine that of Antony, even though he is much younger and has far less military experience, because he has 'natural luck'. This sense of fate no longer smiling upon Antony is strengthened when we hear his soldiers' anxieties that 'his' god, Hercules, has deserted him. The suggestion throughout is that it is not Caesar's rise to power which is the cause of all Antony's misfortunes, it is his lust for Cleopatra. He makes bad military decisions, demoralises his own forces, falls out with his allies, neglects his military responsibilities and spreads disappointment and confusion amongst those who once were his most ardent admirers. By the end of the play Antony has sacrificed personal friendships, authority and power, his marriage, his home, his native citizenship and his life – yet those closest to him will die rather than hurt him, or die in order to join him.

On the other hand, you may sense that Antony leaves Rome in the first place mainly because his luck has run out there and he foresees his influence declining if he stays. Many critics have said that they regard Antony as a paradox and have agreed with Maecenas that he is a character whose 'taints and honours wag'd equal with him'. Antony recognises the demands of duty and of his personal passions, and has his own personal moral code of loyalty to those he values. His 'reputation' is not therefore a purely public matter, (as it would be for Caesar) but is also an expression of how he defines himself. He rails against Caesar precisely because Caesar is prepared to betray personal principles in order to achieve power by any means possible. The 'high Roman fashion' which Cleopatra admires (and after which she follows Antony into death) includes both a private integrity and a sense of public duty which are alien to the likes of Pompey and Caesar.

Unlike other tragic heroes such as Hamlet or Othello, Antony finds no new realisation of self at the end of the play. Nor is he given great soliloquies in which to reflect upon the nature of human kind or its place in the world. Like Hamlet and Othello, he feels a tension between his public or filial obligations and the passions of his heart, but unlike them he does not feel divided within himself by them. In Shakespeare's play Antony is the older, experienced man who, unlike Caesar, recognises that there is more to life than conquest and duty. It is the demands of the outside world which will not let Antony exist content in a world of his own construction, as both warrior and lover; 'My being in Egypt, Caesar,/What was't to you?' (Act 2, scene 2.)

Cleopatra

Like Antony, Cleopatra is a complex and subtle character whose sudden switches of behaviour are often difficult to predict or understand. Caesar may appear to have few emotions and Enobarbus may try to hide his, but Cleopatra often seems to be composed of little else. At the start we see her as a sensual, attractive and highly accomplished courtesan (a royal mistress or prostitute) who has powerful means of attempting to control her lover. She taunts Antony, even insults him, but always with a sexual playfulness which clearly has its effect on him, as Demetrius and Philo observe at the opening of the play. She makes unfair demands on him and criticises him for not loving her enough, whilst he is conscious that he must break away from her bonds or sink to his 'dotage'. This depiction of Cleopatra as an example of the familiar scheming courtesan does not appeal to all critics, some of whom cast her character entirely within the framework of her nobility at the end of the play, but this is to ignore almost all the evidence throughout Acts 1 to 4. Cleopatra herself makes mention of her previous lovers and by the way she does so it seems clear that she became the lover of Pompey and the earlier Caesar, and originally of Antony, because in all three cases she needed the military backing of whoever commanded the conquering power in order to retain her grip on the throne of Egypt. However, her feelings for Antony turn out to be of a different order, and as a mature woman she has seen each of her previous lovers leave her for the Roman Empire and never return. She may worry at the appearance of Octavia because of genuine feelings of insecurity, and Antony's treatment of both his wives could give her little cause for complacency.

Cleopatra is a puzzling and mysterious mix who is simultaneously both seductively appealing and somewhat repellent, as shown by the way many of the Roman characters regard her. Even Antony, who is closer to her than most, is never able to understand or predict her behaviour or motives. She demands to be treated as a general upon the field of battle but ignores military advice, with terrible consequences, and she appears to flirt openly with Caesar's messenger who has come to ask her to betray Antony. Even at the end of the play we are uncertain whether she has played for time in her negotiations with

Caesar in order to attempt to secure an acceptable political solution or only to arrange her own suicide. We might wonder whether she would have taken her own life if Caesar had left her as complete ruler of Egypt. Antony's love for Cleopatra surmounts all these contradictions and more, for it is not of the same kind as is his political marriage to Octavia. In this sense he has no 'reason' for loving Cleopatra, any more than in a materialistic sense, she has any 'reason' to die to be with him at the end.

Cleopatra has a strong comic element to her character and is often witty, even in desperate situations. Her sense of fun is also revealed in the incidents where she recalls how she dressed the drunken Antony in her clothes, or skipped in public through the streets. By the time we reach Act 5 and the death of Antony, we see Cleopatra demonstrate the extent of her love for him – and, it must be admitted, her refusal to become Caesar's prize exhibit – by her determined and noble death at her own hands. By her suicide she follows Antony and transcends defeat, emphasising the nobility of them both and affirming at the same time the extent of their love.

Caesar

In some ways the opposite of Antony, Octavius Caesar is shown as a cold and ambitious young man whose success depends heavily on these aspects of his character. At the start of the play Caesar shares the rule of the Roman Empire with Antony and Lepidus, but by the end of the action he has defeated them both to become sole ruler. He sees himself as ushering in a 'time of universal peace' (Act 4, scene 6), an idea which would have been immediately recognised by the audience of Shakespeare's time for the dramatic irony it is. The historical Caesar's reign was perceived by the Elizabethans as ushering in a long period of military and civil peace which had been ordained by God in preparation for the coming of Christ. The character of Caesar in the play reflects this view of history, which is why we see him drawn as dignified, majestic and somewhat aloof and mysterious to the other characters. Caesar is calculating, manipulative and dispassionate where Antony is wilful and generous and seems at the mercy both of his own misjudgements and of events around him. The swiftness of Caesar's victories is a puzzle to Canidius (Act 3, scene 7) where his rapid progress 'carries beyond belief'; he wins many of his battles despite Antony's best efforts, as fate seems to play into his hands; even Antony's guardian spirit is intimidated by Caesar according to the soothsayer in Act 2, scene 3: 'near him, thy angel/Becomes afeared ; as being o'erpower'd'. But Caesar is not a pleasant character; he breaks the treaty with Pompey, betrays Lepidus, is content for political reasons to see his sister married to Antony in spite of his feelings about him; and forces all Antony's deserters into the front line of battle to be killed first. But neither is Caesar heartless and without feelings; he cares for his sister and can even appreciate Antony's finer qualities; he openly admires Antony's achievements and the nobility of the deaths of the lovers at the end of the play. But it is Caesar's lack of susceptibility to his own passions which most separates him from both Cleopatra and Antony. This also marks him off from the other military leaders and their advisers, as we see at the end of Act 2 when only he retains a longer perspective on their military planning and declines further drink on Pompey's ship.

As a representative of the military and political power of Rome, Caesar is contrasted against Cleopatra, whose life is driven by passions. He manipulates her and lies to her because of his determination to humiliate her by exhibiting her in Rome as an example of his own achievements and a demonstration of the might of the Empire. Although Caesar is left at the end of the play in complete control of the mortal and physical world, the significance of Cleopatra's spiritual victory over death would not have been lost on the play's original audiences.

Charmian

Cleopatra talks to Charmian much more than to her two other ladies-in-waiting, Iras and Alexas, and also shares with her far more intimate thoughts. Many of Charmian's comments contain references to lust and sexual allusions, which highlight the supposedly voluptuous and self-indulgent character of the Egyptian court. The soothsayer tells Charmian that she will be 'fairer' in the future, will love more than she will be loved, and will live longer than Cleopatra. All three predictions seem to come true, for Charmian's love for and loyalty to Cleopatra know no bounds and she dies after Cleopatra. She is touchingly protective of her mistress, even straightening Cleopatra's royal head-dress after her death to ensure that she continues to look regal. In an attempt to help her mistress, Charmian suggests that Cleopatra should pretend to commit suicide in order to win Antony round from his anger at her. Whilst this is the kind of tactic which Cleopatra has used on earlier occasions to get her way, here it misfires badly. The ill-fated message reaches Antony, who mortally wounds himself in his grief before the truth can arrive. But Charmian can also be a soothing influence on her mistress, as when she persuades Cleopatra not to harm further the messenger who brings her news of Antony's sudden marriage to Octavia. Charmian is a spirited young woman whose fun-loving, pleasure-seeking ways reflect those of Cleopatra, as does her eventual fate. She is, like her mistress, imaginative, theatrical and intensely loyal to those she loves.

Enobarbus

As Antony's chief officer, closest adviser and friend, Enobarbus should stay loyally next to his master's side. His eventual desertion, therefore, especially when Antony responds to it with generosity and self-criticism, proves too much for his sense of honour and he dies in the enemy camp, a broken-hearted man. The desertion of Enobarbus is an example in the play of why it is unwise to allow one's head to rule one's heart – for Enobarbus leaves Antony because of the latter's passionate involvement with Cleopatra. Enobarbus thinks his friend's love affair has softened his will, corrupted his judgement and led them to several military defeats. In this Enobarbus echoes the thinking outlined at the start of the play by Caesar. But eventually Enobarbus concludes that loyalty is more valuable than good sense and this forms an important illustration – along with the final deaths of Antony and Cleopatra – of the play's treatment of power and love. Enobarbus does not desert Antony because he dislikes him but because he can no longer bear the sight of his friend and master degenerating into a shadow of his former glory, and because he thinks that this degeneration has made defeat inevitable.

On a number of occasions Enobarbus performs the function of a chorus, commenting bluntly and cynically on the action of the play – as when in Act 2, scene 2, he mocks Lepidus for his simultaneous fawning over both Caesar and Antony. His gruff soldier's manner makes for much of the humour in the play and his is often the only voice of reason. He is highly critical of Antony's behaviour with Cleopatra, although he does not blame her for what happens, and it is he who describes her first meeting with Antony in beautifully poetic terms. Until his death, Enobarbus is present on every important occasion in the play. He constantly offers Antony sound military advice; he exhibits the wise judgement of an experienced campaigner until he is overtaken by his distress about what is happening to Antony. Like Cleopatra's lady-in-waiting, Iras, Enobarbus dies of broken-hearted grief; both being overcome by the torment of their situation, both loving the one they most wished to serve.

Octavia

Although only present in the action for a brief period, Octavia acts as a revealing foil to Cleopatra, who is both curious about and jealous of Antony's new wife. A model of the Roman qualities of obedience and duty, Octavia is torn between her duty to her husband Antony and to her brother Caesar. Although used by her brother as a political pawn to seal the truce between him and Antony, there is nothing to suggest that Octavia is anything other than a loyal and loving wife to Antony. Her unannounced arrival in Rome offends Caesar and whilst it may well suit Caesar's intentions to become enraged at his sister's apparent rejection, it may be that his feelings of brotherly affection are genuinely affronted. Enobarbus correctly foresees that Octavia will only increase Antony's love for Cleopatra and Octavia's eventual disappearance from the action during Act 3 is hardly noticed.

Themes and images in *Antony and Cleopatra*

Order and discipline

Order and discipline

The play opens with a heated discussion contrasting the Roman discipline of a soldier's duty with the attractions of emotional and sexual gratification. Caesar and Lepidus represent the purely Roman view of the importance of order and discipline when they compare Antony's previous nobility and achievements to his present neglect of his duty. Antony's soldiers think he is making a fool of himself, but he sees himself reaching a 'new heaven' through his love for Cleopatra. Soldierly duty and the appeal of 'lascivious wassails' are both seen to be extremes; Antony is torn between the demands of military power and his need for emotional and physical satisfaction, whilst Cleopatra seems to have discharged her political responsibilities through the manipulation of luxury and passion.

Antony ignores his duty at the start of the play by refusing to hear the messages from Rome, but later realises that his idleness and preoccupation with love is allowing 'ten thousand harms, more than the ills I know' to grow. When part of his territory is successfully invaded, he decides that he must break away from Cleopatra. Order and discipline are shown to be essential for society to exist, a common theme in many of Shakespeare's plays and a preoccupation of the contemporary times.

At the end of the play it is Caesar who commands the stage and his closing speech underlines the military and political victory which he has gained. Although Caesar acknowledges 'a pair so famous' as Antony and Cleopatra, his words do not glorify their transcendent love, but set it in its earthly context. The central theme of the play has been variously interpreted as a romance about how immortal love can conquer all circumstances, even death; and as a cautionary tale about the risks of neglecting the discipline of duty. Does the play show the scheming courtesan Cleopatra and the cold military strategist Antony being transformed by love? Or is Antony a weak and foolish man who is seduced and exploited because of his desire for sexual gratification? Is the death of Cleopatra brought about by her defeat at the hands of Caesar, which leaves suicide as the only realistic course open to her? Or is her death an affirmation of her love for Antony, a turning away from the pleasures of the world, and her refusal to be parted from him? The play may therefore be seen to have two separate climaxes at the end of Act 5, one in the physical, military and political world and the other in the personal and spiritual world.

Closely associated with the themes of order and discipline in the play are considerations of loyalty and betrayal. Examples of loyalty to a master, a friend or a lover appear in different guises: the loyalty of Enobarbus to Antony; the love of Antony for Cleopatra; the love of Iras, Charmian and Eros for their masters; and so on. The conflicts between worldly power and spiritual glory are often emphasised by references to the contrasts between gods and humans, the search for peace in the struggle between life and death, and the conflicting appeals of the victories of war and the fulfilment of love. There are many examples of the way upholding one loyalty often involves betraying another, as when Antony's loyalty to Cleopatra involves his betrayal of his soldierly duty to Rome and to Caesar. Enobarbus deserts Antony because of his own loyalty to a Roman code of ethics which values soldierly duty and military conquest above personal love, but he is distraught when he realises that Antony's personal love and regard for him is undiminished. But although upholding personal loyalty which is rooted in love for another may not require betrayal, it often demands great sacrifice, as when the closest servants of both Antony and Cleopatra give their lives out of loyalty. Individual love for and loyalty to another is celebrated as a spiritual goal which should be held above the loyalties of office and duty. Cleopatra emphasises the spiritual essence of the individual when she cries: 'I am fire, and air' as she prepares for her own death.

Love and pleasure

Love and pleasure

Although much criticised for his behaviour by others, Antony chooses the pleasures of love over the appeal of military conquest and political power. Although his character contains elements of both, he ultimately chooses Egypt over Rome. At the end of the play Antony and Cleopatra's love for each other transcends the physical world, from which their deaths free them, and exists in a spiritual paradise, a god-like existence 'past the size of dreaming'. Whilst order and discipline are essential for social order and cohesion, the spiritual and physical intensity of love is more fulfilling for the individual: at the end of the play, Cleopatra can be seen to be transformed by her love for Antony. After Antony's death the opposition of love and duty represented by Egypt and Rome is sharpened by the concentration of the action on the fates of Cleopatra and Caesar. Most of the imagery about Rome and Roman virtues is associated with control, discipline or moderation, whilst that associated with Egypt is about sensuality, excesses, overflowing and melting.

The world

The world

The imagery of the play is full of references to the world, the heavens, the ocean, the sun, moon, stars and vastness in general. These are used to emphasise the play's concern with grandeur, luxury and magnificence but are especially effective in creating an impression of the main characters as creatures so awesome in size and power that they dwarf the world and all its concerns. Octavia describes how devastating the strife between Antony and Caesar is likely to be: 'Wars 'twixt you twain would be/As if the world should cleave'. Later, Cleopatra, talking about the state to which the dead Antony has risen, speaks of a creature whose 'legs bestrid the ocean'. References also abound to nature: from flies, gnats, snakes and the crocodile to the power of storms, the majestic heavens and the beauties of the world; these are variously used to emphasise the power and mystery of the world and the richness of sensual delight to be found in its teeming life and vibrant energy. Many of these references appear in conjunction with Antony and Cleopatra, or in the scenes set in Egypt.

Text commentary

Act 1 Scene 1

Philo and Demetrius discuss how Antony's involvement with Queen Cleopatra is causing him to ignore his military responsibilities. When news arrives from Rome, Cleopatra enters with Antony and taunts him about how much he actually loves her. She suggests that the news may be messages commanding him to return to Rome, either from Fulvia, his wife, or from Octavius Caesar, his comrade. Antony replies that he does not care about the messages; he wants to stay with Cleopatra in Egypt. He tells her they should not argue but go for a walk through the streets instead to see how the ordinary people are living their lives. Antony does not, therefore, attend to the messages.

**'Nay, but this dotage of our general's
O'erflows the measure...'**

Many times in the play Antony is compared to a great colossus or god. Here, Philo remembers how Antony's eyes 'have glow'd like plated Mars' when looking over battlefields in the past. These first few words of the play also have to do with the 'o'erflowing' which characterises everything to do with Egypt: contrasting with everything Roman, which is typified in its attitude to the former by the first word uttered: 'Nay'.

Antony

**'Here is my space,
Kingdoms are clay: our dungy earth alike
Feeds beast as man...'**

Love and pleasure

Antony recognises that he belongs in Egypt and that the conquest of empires means only the acquisition of 'dungy earth', in contrast to the world of the imagination and sensual excess which the lovers inhabit. This contrast between the two different worlds of Rome and Egypt appears on many occasions throughout the action.

**'Fie, wrangling queen!
Whom every thing becomes, to chide, to laugh,
To weep...'**

Part in frustration, part in affection, Antony chastises Cleopatra for her ability to turn every passion into something fair, to be admired. She has always used

her charms to manipulate others to great effect – later Antony in his fury describes her as a 'witch'. Several times Cleopatra finds herself in situations where this is the key which she uses to get her own way, whether it be a matter here of teasing Antony or, later, of securing her own death in order to avoid becoming Caesar's slave.

Act 1 Scene 2

The soothsayer (a fortune-teller) talks to Cleopatra's ladies-in-waiting and tells them that they will both live longer than Cleopatra and see less happy times in the future. As Charmian and Iras laugh about this with another servant, Alexas, Cleopatra arrives. When she sees Antony coming she says she will not speak to him, and leaves. Antony attends to the messages from Rome and discovers that his wife Fulvia has battled with his brother Lucius, after which they both united to fight Octavius Caesar, but were defeated. Antony is angry with himself when he also learns that the Parthians (frequent enemies of Rome) have conquered a large piece of Roman territory in his absence. Another messenger tells Antony that Fulvia has died on her way to see him. Feeling guilty that he recently wished his wife dead, Antony decides to be free of Cleopatra. He tells Enobarbus he will return to Rome to help Caesar fight the rebel Pompey, and Enobarbus jokes about the trouble this will cause with Cleopatra.

'In nature's infinite book of secrecy A little I can read.'

The soothsayer introduces the idea (which runs throughout the play) that nature is a repository of mystery and power of which mortals see and understand little. It is into this mysterious world that Antony and Cleopatra eventually enter, because of their love for each other. The conversation of the women, though amusing, light-hearted and witty, soon turns to a discussion of sensuous pleasure, sexual gratification, procreation and the whims of fortune. These are key ideas surrounding Cleopatra, who enters here, although it is significant that the women mistake her for Antony at first, hearing approaching footsteps and assuming it is Antony. This subtle touch anticipates the way the two main characters move towards becoming one as the play progresses.

The world

'You shall be more beloving than belov'd.'

The soothsayer's words anticipate the outcome of the play and summarise the essential, paradoxical motive for the deaths of the two lovers. His language here also illustrates that prose is not always given to the 'baser' characters in the play, or used only for comedy. Throughout *Antony and Cleopatra*, we see poetry and prose intermingled. Blank verse comprises most of the play, and most characters' speech, with differences being concentrated most often in the imagery used in the Roman and Egyptian worlds. Enobarbus uses prose in a complex and sophisticated way, often setting the comments of others against a particular context or background. In the second scene of the next act, for example, he interrupts the triumvirs' conversation with home truths so often that Antony is obliged to tell him bluntly to shut up. On other occasions Enobarbus changes from prose to poetry, as when he describes Cleopatra's barge on the river Cydnus.

'If every of your wishes had a womb,
And fertile every wish, a million.'

The world

The soothsayer summarises the luxurious, fertile, sensuous life of Egypt which symbolises the life force within the world of nature, in contrast to the rigid and sterile world of Rome. Egypt is therefore upheld as a representation of emotional, creative forces; Rome of the denial necessary for military conquest and political power.

***Ant.* 'She is cunning past man's thought.'**
***Eno.* 'Alack, sir, no, her passions are made of nothing but the finest part of pure love.'**

It is difficult to know whether Antony or Enobarbus here most accurately sums up the essential nature of Cleopatra. We see her manipulation of Antony, Caesar, servants and messengers alike. We hear of how she has used her skills as a courtesan in the past to preserve her throne and power. Yet Enobarbus, who has here fallen under Cleopatra's spell, offers an important insight into understanding the action and ending of the play.

Enobarbus

Act 1 Scene 3

Although Charmian suggests to Cleopatra that she should support Antony's decision to return to Rome if she wants to keep his love, Cleopatra is moody and difficult as Antony tries several times to tell her of his decision. However, when she realises that she risks going too far and that Antony is determined, she wishes him well and he assures her of his love.

'If you find him sad,
Say I am dancing; if in mirth, report
That I am sudden sick...'

Cleopatra's first words in the play – 'If it be love indeed, tell me how much' – revealed that she has a shrewd knowledge of how to capture and keep a man's affections. Here she tells Charmian that if she behaved otherwise, she would risk losing Antony, and she seems genuinely concerned to prevent

Cleopatra

this. At this stage in the play we may not be sure whether Cleopatra needs Antony for political reasons or whether her love for him is genuine; the latter appears to be so by the end of the play. Should we interpret her tormenting of him as a lovers' game or as a means of retaining control of him, and should we regard her many letters to him when he leaves for Rome in the same way? It seems difficult to understand why, if she truly loves Antony, she should provoke him so deliberately. Later in the play her behaviour during the battles enrages Antony to the point where she has to flee for her life, pleading that she did not expect her actions to result in his defeat. On these occasions we could be observing the powerful ebb and flow of a passionate love-affair, where each lover is unable to exist without the other and emotions run high as Cleopatra tries to ensure that Antony will remain with her. Or we could be witnessing Antony trying to work out a situation in which he finds himself fatally torn between his soldierly duties to the state and his feelings as a human being.

Love and pleasure

At the start of the play, Cleopatra seems always to be probing Antony's responses for weak spots, reminding him of his public and personal responsibilities in a way which seems designed to encourage him to shake them off. In this amusing exchange here, Antony can barely get a word in as she accuses him of thinking little of her and of being fickle in his affections.

'Thy soldier, servant, making peace or war,
As thou affects.'

Antony says he is wholly the servant of Cleopatra's wishes. Later, we see how this becomes literally true as he follows her wishes out of love for her, even when his military judgement tells him he is committing folly.

Act 1 Scene 4

Caesar tells Lepidus about Antony's 'disgusting' and soft life in Egypt and of his depraved behaviour with Cleopatra. News arrives that Pompey's strength is rising and that he is now helped by two pirates, Menecrates and Menas, who are threatening the Italian coasts. Caesar hopes that Antony will return to being the valiant general he has been famous for and will help them.

'You shall find there
A man who is the abstract of all faults
That all men follow.'

Caesar's first words in the play are about his displeasure at the excesses of

Caesar

Antony, whose loss of judgement and masculinity are more than once compared unflatteringly to his past greatness. But here, when a messenger arrives with news that the rebel Pompey is gathering support from those who feared Caesar most, Caesar does not blame himself but instead comments that the common people are fickle. He notes that those who have risen to power on a wave of popular support often see this wane until they fall; then they are once again loved by the crowd. Caesar does not see Antony in terms of his observation that 'the ebb'd man, ne'er lov'd till ne'er worth love,/Comes dear'd, by being lack'd', although it is an apt description of Antony's rise and fall.

Order and discipline

'Antony, Leave thy lascivious wassails.'

Caesar praises Antony's past military achievements in terms which depict him as a god-like creature, who was able to drink water which 'beasts would cough at' and could live off 'the roughest berry, on the rudest hedge' or eat 'the barks of trees'. Whilst crossing the Alps he 'didst eat strange flesh,/Which some did die to look on' and bore it all 'like a soldier'. At at the end of the play Caesar remains supreme ruler of this physical world of military conquest and suffering, to which he is fettered, whilst Antony rises beyond it into the world as represented by Egypt; a world of imagination, sensuousness, mythology and legend.

Antony

Act 1 Scene 5

In Alexandria, Cleopatra longs for Antony and sends messengers every day to tell him how much she loves him. Charmian risks punishment when she reminds Cleopatra that she once felt just the same about Julius Caesar when he was in Egypt years before, but Cleopatra dismisses this and says her love for Antony is more mature and true.

'I take no pleasure In aught an eunuch has...'

Cleopatra pretends to envy Mardian, the eunuch, because of his lack of sexual desire, for hers has made her long to 'sleep out this great gap of time/My Antony is away'. But Mardian declares that he has 'fierce affections' and often thinks of Venus and Mars. This mythological reference, like many in the play, reflects directly upon the main action, for Venus was the sensual goddess of love who became the paramour of Mars, the god of war. *Antony and Cleopatra* is one of Shakespeare's most bawdy and sensual plays, containing many references to swords in general,

Love and pleasure

and Antony's sword in particular, as symbols of military and sexual potency. Here Cleopatra says she desires to 'drink mandragora', the juice of the mandrake plant. This juice has strong anaesthetic qualities and the mandrake plant itself resembles a man's legs or sexual organs. Mardian's castrated condition is therefore a reminder to Cleopatra of the pleasures of which Antony's absence deprives her.

' "Where's my serpent of old Nile?"
For so he calls me.'

In an interesting anticipation of the play's ending, Cleopatra acknowledges her affinity in Antony's eyes with the asps of the Nile. The asp's poison is swift, bringing a narcotic sleep, just as Antony's excess of passionate love for the sensuous Cleopatra intoxicates him, and they both end in death. Here Cleopatra counts both the sun and death amongst her lovers, a reference she repeats after she applies the second asp to her arm in the second scene of Act 5.

Self-test Questions Act 1

Uncover the plot

Delete two of the three alternatives given, to find the correct plot. Beware possible misconceptions and muddles.

In Egypt/Rome/Alexandria two friends of Antony's talk about how his involvement with Queen Cleopatra is causing him to ignore his military responsibilities. When news arrives from Rome/Cyprus/Actium, Cleopatra taunts Antony that this may be a message from Octavia/Fulvia/Alexas or from Caesar/Ptolemy/Pompey. Antony says he will stay in Egypt/return to Rome/read the messages later. A soothsayer foretells the futures of Seleucus/Mardian/Charmian and Diomedes/Iras/Alexas. Antony learns that his sister/wife/cousin has battled with his brother/son-in-law/father, after which they have both fought Caesar, who has been victorious/careless/defeated. Antony also learns that the Syrians/Egyptians/Parthians have conquered Roman territory. Another messenger tells him that his wife/sister/son has died. Antony decides to return to Rome and help Caesar fight Pompey/Ptolemy/Proculeius. Cleopatra is happy/unhappy/resigned about this. Caesar tells Lepidus/Varrius/Gallus about Antony's life in Egypt. News arrives that his enemy is now helped by Silius/Menecrates/Maecenas and Demetrius/Canidius/Menas, who are robbers/pirates/soldiers. Cleopatra sends messengers to Antony every hour/day/week to tell him how much she loves him. Iras/Charmian/Alexas reminds Cleopatra that she once loved Caesar/Pompey/Ptolemy just as much, years before.

Who? What? Why? When? Where? How?

1 Who tells Cleopatra that they have met 'twenty several' of her messengers, and where were these messengers going and why?
2 According to whom, who ate strange flesh and why?
3 When the messengers first arrive from Rome, what news does Cleopatra tell Antony they may have brought?

4 According to the news he receives from Alexandria, what inappropriate behaviour does Caesar say that Antony is indulging in?
5 Who asks whom for mandragora and why?
6 Cleopatra congratulates Mardian on being free from what, and why is Mardian free of it?
7 Who calls whom a 'serpent of old Nile'?
8 According to Philo, into what will Antony – whom he calls 'the triple pillar of the world' – become transformed if he does not soon change his behaviour?
9 Who says that Antony's heart has now 'become the bellows and the fan/To cool a gypsy's lust'?
10 Which three specific things does the soothsayer foretell for Charmian?

Who said that, and to whom?

1 'Go, you wild bedfellow, you cannot soothsay.'
2 'Things that are past are done, with me.'
3 'Pompey/Thrives in our idleness.'
4 'Nay, but this dotage of our general's/O'erflows the measure.'
5 'This grief is crown'd with consolation, your old smock brings forth a new petticoat.'
6 'In time we hate that which we often fear.'
7 'I will give thee bloody teeth.'
8 'O then we bring forth weeds,/When our quick minds lie still.'
9 'You think of him too much.'
10 'Fulvia thy wife is dead.'

Open quotes

Identify the scene; complete the phrase; identify the speaker and the character being spoken to.

1 'Think on me,/That I am with Phoebus' amorous pinches black,'
2 'She is cunning past man's thought.' (Answered by a second speaker)
3 'These strong Egyptian fetters I must break…'
4 'If every of your wishes had a womb…'
5 'I must from this enchanting queen break off…'
6 'Here is my space,/Kingdoms are clay:'
7 'In each thing give him way, cross him in nothing.' (Answered by a second speaker)
8 'Our slippery people,/Whose love is never link'd…'
9 'Under a compelling occasion let women die: it were pity to cast them away for nothing,…'
10 'Now I see, I see,/In Fulvia's death,'

Act 2 Scene 1

In Messina (Sicily), Sextus Pompey talks to the pirates Menecrates and Menas about how he feels confident of beating Caesar and Lepidus. This confidence is shattered when the worrying news arrives that Antony has left Egypt for Rome. Pompey realises that this could make things much more difficult for him, although he continues to hope for the best.

'We, ignorant of ourselves, Beg often our own harms…'

Menecrates advises Pompey, with unconscious irony, that the gods often deny humankind its wishes in order to protect it from itself. Pompey craves greater power, which later he is denied by the treachery of Caesar.

Act 2 Scene 2

In Rome, Lepidus is preparing to host the meeting between Antony and Caesar and asks Enobarbus to help him ensure that Antony speaks gently. Enobarbus says that Antony will do as he pleases. When Antony and Caesar arrive, Antony insists that he had nothing to do with the rebellion of his wife and brother. He adds that he is sorry he did not respond to Caesar's messages for help, because he was recovering from drinking and because he had fallen into decadent ways in Egypt. Caesar and Antony agree to put the matter behind them and unite to fight Pompey. As a symbol of their alliance, Antony agrees to marry Octavia, Caesar's sister. After Antony and Caesar leave to discuss the wedding, Enobarbus tells Maecenas and Agrippa about Egypt and the beautiful Cleopatra. He says that Antony will never leave her.

'That truth should be silent, I had almost forgot.'

As Antony's close friend and trusted adviser, Enobarbus is given considerable freedom in what he may safely say. At the start of this scene Enobarbus makes it plain to Lepidus that he has not the slightest intention of trying to constrain what Antony might say and that he, like his master, will 'answer like himself'. Following Antony's request that he 'speak no more', Enobarbus responds fearlessly with the quotation heading this paragraph.

'Age cannot wither her, nor custom stale Her infinite variety...'

In a move directed by political duty rather than by passion, Antony agrees to marry Caesar's sister, Octavia. Immediately afterwards, Enobarbus here describes to Agrippa and Maecenas the first meeting of Cleopatra and Antony. The contrast between the two women could not be more sharp, for Octavia cannot hope to compete with a creature of such overpowering sensuousness as we find in the words of Enobarbus. The culmination of the description of Cleopatra's introduction to Antony sums up her powerful allure. Enobarbus stresses her magical sensuous appearance; even the water of the river was 'amorous' of her boat's oars; she was like the goddess Venus surrounded by mythical creatures; her boat itself burned with the sun's fire, illuminating the surrounding world of nature with life. Everything about her fanned the appetite of the senses and Enobarbus says that Antony can never leave her now, for 'she makes hungry,/ Where most she satisfies.' Note, however, that Enobarbus's words consist of

exaggerated language about the sensuous excesses of Egypt, and may serve more to generate an effect on the hearers than to tell the literal truth.

Act 2 Scene 3

Antony asks his new wife, Octavia, for her understanding when he is away and promises to behave well, in spite of his previous bad reputation. Octavia goes to bed and the soothsayer comes in and tells Antony that Caesar's fortunes will rise higher than his; Antony should therefore return to Egypt. Even though he has just married Octavia, Antony decides to return to Egypt and Cleopatra.

'I' the east my pleasure lies.'

The soothsayer has just advised Antony that his protecting angel is frightened and overpowered when he is close to Caesar and that he will only be worthy when he is away from Caesar. Here Antony makes the decision to return to Egypt. But is this because he is deeply troubled by what the soothsayer has just said? Some critics have argued for this view, pointing to Antony's resentment of the younger Caesar – and to his later challenge of hand-to-hand combat with him – as evidence of the personal insecurity of a character who fears for his status as one of the three rulers of the Roman Empire. Other writers feel that Antony leaves because he has nothing in Rome to hold him; they argue that his marriage to Octavia is merely a matter of political convenience to keep the peace, not a marriage of love, whilst his passion for Cleopatra is genuine. A third alternative could be that Caesar is right (in Act 1, scene 4) in seeing Antony as a fallen man composed of the most extreme faults, who has lost the heart of a soldier and prefers to amuse himself fishing, drinking with slaves and spending time in Cleopatra's bed.

Antony

Some critics who have taken this latter position have seen Antony as an artistic soul who enjoys the rich sensuality of life, unlike Caesar, who cannot allow himself even to enjoy Pompey's shipboard party. Yet another group see Antony as a moody, irresponsible depressive, a self-pitying and self-indulgent character who seems set on his own destruction. Deciding why Antony leaves Rome at this time may help you form your personal view of him. Caution is needed, however, as Antony is not a simple character and his actions are often difficult to explain – even those closest to him are often confused by the way he acts.

Love and pleasure

Act 2 Scene 4

A very short scene in which Maecenas, Lepidus and Agrippa prepare to leave Rome and to meet Caesar and Antony at Misenum for the campaign against Pompey.

Act 2 Scene 5

Cleopatra, waiting in Alexandria, hears of Antony and Octavia's marriage and becomes furious at the news, attacking the messenger. She says she does not want to see Antony again, but tells Alexas to ask the messenger about Octavia's appearance.

'Ere the ninth hour, I drunk him to his bed; Then put my tires and mantles on him...'

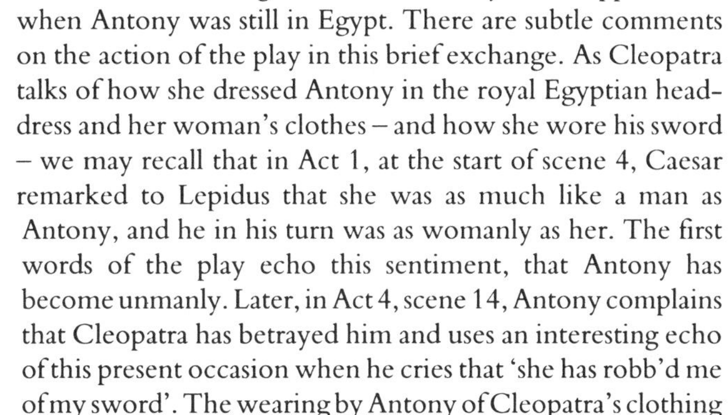

Cleopatra and her ladies-in-waiting share the memory of a happier time when Antony was still in Egypt. There are subtle comments on the action of the play in this brief exchange. As Cleopatra talks of how she dressed Antony in the royal Egyptian headdress and her woman's clothes – and how she wore his sword – we may recall that in Act 1, at the start of scene 4, Caesar remarked to Lepidus that she was as much like a man as Antony, and he in his turn was as womanly as her. The first words of the play echo this sentiment, that Antony has become unmanly. Later, in Act 4, scene 14, Antony complains that Cleopatra has betrayed him and uses an interesting echo of this present occasion when he cries that 'she has robb'd me of my sword'. The wearing by Antony of Cleopatra's clothing and royal headdress also foretells the action in Act 3, scene 6, where we learn that he has behaved as though Egypt had conquered Rome – not the other way round – and given away large parts of the Roman Empire to Cleopatra and her children. Several times in the play we find Antony's judgement deferring to that of Cleopatra, as though he had become the unthinking instrument of her will.

'Some innocents 'scape not the thunderbolt...'

Cleopatra's fiery temper is illustrated here in a way which cleverly anticipates the messenger's second visit in Act 3, scene 3. Here the messenger makes the mistake of being direct about his news of Antony: 'Madam, he's married to Octavia'. Cleopatra at once strikes him and attacks him violently. Aware of the licence which her power grants her, she draws a knife on the messenger, who flees for his life, only returning with the greatest caution. The humour injected into this and its associated scene later skilfully emphasises the tempestuous feelings of Cleopatra and underlines her unpredictable and passionate nature. The scene also introduces the knife which Cleopatra carries, which will become dramatically important later, as will the serpents to which she refers. Her words are also somewhat ironic, for in some ways both she and Antony are 'innocents' destroyed by the political and emotional thunderbolts around them.

Act 2 Scene 6

Pompey recognises that he is not strong enough to defeat the others now that Antony is on their side and meets Caesar, Lepidus and Antony to agree a truce. They decide to hold a feast together to celebrate their treaty. Enobarbus remains behind and talks to Menas, saying that he thinks Antony will leave Octavia for Cleopatra.

'But you shall find the band that seems to tie their friendship together will be the very strangler of their amity.'

Octavia

Enobarbus correctly recognises that the 'holy, cold, and still' character of Octavia will not satisfy Antony for long. He sees that Antony is a man of passion and imagination, although he (perhaps surprisingly) fails to anticipate Antony's reaction to his own desertion later.

'He will to his Egyptian dish again...'

Enobarbus continues the use of sensuous food imagery which appears often in the play, from Cleopatra describing herself (Act 1, scene 5) as a 'morsel for a monarch' to the way Julius Caesar 'grew fat with feasting' in Egypt. Even Cleopatra's clown at the end of the play understands that 'a woman is a dish for the gods'. Although the Roman characters in the play usually refer to the connection between the sensual pleasures of eating and sex in disparaging terms, the Egyptian characters relish both.

Love and pleasure

Act 2 Scene 7

During the banquet on Pompey's ship, Lepidus is teased by the other leaders. Menas takes Pompey to one side and suggests that now he should cut the throats of the three others. Pompey tells him that he should have done it first and told him afterwards, but now he knows about it in advance he cannot agree to it. Menas is bitter at this and decides that he will leave Pompey's service. The generals become more drunk and start to dance and sing, until Caesar declares that such behaviour does not suit their serious business. They all leave, as the celebrations cease.

'Your serpent of Egypt is bred now of your mud by the operation of your sun: so is your crocodile.'

The world

Lepidus echoes a common belief in Shakespeare's time, that the action of the sun can produce life from dead matter. Significantly for the imagery and thematic structure of the play, we can see the mysterious powers of nature regenerating life from base matter as a parallel to the transformation which happens to Antony and Cleopatra, as they transcend the base considerations of the earthly realm at the end of the play.

'And though thou think me poor, I am the man Will give thee all the world.'

Menas suggests to Pompey that if the throats of the others are cut whilst they are drunk on his ship, Pompey will be left as sole ruler. Although Pompey rejects this idea, it is noticeable that he does so only because Menas has sought to involve him in the initial decision to act, which would taint his honour, *not* because he is averse to the idea. Pompey would have been glad to accept the deed, once done, and Menas's resentment at Pompey's attitude is a result of this knowledge. Politics and power are frequently set against pleasure and passion throughout the action of the play. Caesar's betrayal of Lepidus and his treacherous attack on Pompey serve to help determine the fates of Antony and Cleopatra just as much as the lovers' passions shape events in the outside world.

Order and discipline

Self-test Questions Act 2

Uncover the plot

Delete two of the three alternatives given, to find the correct plot. Beware possible misconceptions and muddles.

Pompey is based in Misenum/Messina/Actium and feels confident/uncertain/depressed about his chances of winning the coming battles. News arrives that Antony/Caesar/Lepidus is travelling to Alexandria/Rome/Athens. Lepidus/Demetrius/Scarus asks Thidias/Enobarbus/Menecrates to help him with the meeting between Pompey/Caesar/Varrius and Antony. Antony says he had no/some/a major involvement in the rebellion of his sister/cousin/wife and son/father/brother. Antony says he did not respond to messages for help because he was angry/had a hangover/did not receive them. They agree to unite to fight Lepidus/Pompey/Ptolemy. Antony agrees to marry Caesar's daughter/cousin/sister, Fulvia/Octavia/Decretia. Enobarbus/Menecrates/Charmian says Antony will never leave Cleopatra. Although just married, Antony decides his future lies in Syria/Messina/Alexandria. Caesar and Antony are to meet at Misenum/Messina/Actium for the campaign against Pompey.

Cleopatra hears of the marriage of Antony and is amused/furious/indifferent at the news. Pompey, Caesar, Lepidus and Antony meet to agree where to fight/to exchange prisoners/a truce. During a banquet on Caesar's/Antony's/Pompey's ship Menas/Gallus/Scarus suggests to Lepidus/Caesar/Pompey that they should cut the throats of the others. This plan does not work because it is discovered/rejected/badly executed. The generals enjoy themselves at the feast until Caesar/Antony/Lepidus says that this behaviour does not suit their serious business.

Who? What? Why? When? Where? How?

1 Why does Enobarbus jokingly say that the attendant who carries off the drunken Lepidus is a strong fellow?

2 Who warns Antony not to stay by Caesar's side?
3 According to Enobarbus, how did Cleopatra first meet Antony?
4 Who tells whom that he is the man who can give him all the world?
5 In Scene 2, where does Caesar say that Pompey and his forces are based?
6 What thing – and according to whom – is shaped like itself, is 'as broad as it hath breadth' and moves by its own organs?
7 What specific (but erroneous)reasons did Pompey have for thinking that he had an advantage over each of his three opponents?
8 What reason does Antony give Caesar for Fulvia's war on him?
9 How is peace sealed between Caesar and Antony and what reason is given for thinking that this measure will be effective?
10 What (rather hypocritical) reason does Pompey give Menas for refusing his offer to cut the others' throats?

Who said that and about whom?

1 '... our courteous... ,/Whom ne'er the word of 'No' woman heard speak.'
2 'The world, and my great office, will sometimes/Divide me from your bosom.'
3 '...entreat your captain/To soft and gentle speech.'
4 '...vilest things become themselves in her;'
5 'I have heard that Julius Caesar/Grew fat with feasting there.'
6 'Melt Egypt into Nile! and kindly creatures/Turn all into serpents!'
7 'We, ignorant of ourselves,/Beg often our own harms.'
8 'He will to his Egyptian dish again.'
9 'If thou dost play with him at any game,/Thou art sure to lose.'
10 'The people love me, and the sea is mine.'

Open quotes

Identify the scene; complete the phrase; identify the speaker and the character being spoken to.

1 'Your serpent of Egypt is bred now of your mud by...'
2 'I will to Egypt:/And though I make this marriage for my peace,'
3 'Who seeks and will not take, when once 'tis offer'd, ...'
4 'Age cannot wither her, nor custom stale...' (Complete next three lines).
5 'But you shall find the band that seems to tie their friendship together...'
6 'Royal wench!/She made great Caesar lay his sword...'
7 'We look not for Mark Antony here: pray you, is he married to Cleopatra?'
8 'Let me cut the cable,/And when we are put off...'
9 'I did not think to draw my sword 'gainst Pompey,/For he hath laid...'
10 'I did not think/This amorous surfeiter would have donn'd his helm/For such a petty war:'

Act 3 Scene 1

An army of the Parthians has been defeated by Venditius, Antony's general. Venditius tells Silius that he will not chase the retreating army to gain a greater victory, in case Antony might feel overshadowed. Venditius warns Silius of the dangers of too much success, saying that Antony may not be pleased if they seem to be more successful than him and may withhold promotion from them. Instead, Venditius will write to Antony and tell him how, in his name, they have defeated the Parthians. They will then go to join him in Athens.

'Better to leave undone, than by our deed
Acquire too high a fame...'

Order and discipline

Ventidius advises Silius against achieving too much, for fear it may attract the attention of their master, who may become jealous. This is an interesting reversal of the traditional Roman code of honour, and reflects upon the credit taken by both Antony and Caesar for actions done in their name. Ventidius shows himself a shrewd judge of others.

Act 3 Scene 2

As Antony prepares to leave Rome, the suspicious Caesar cautions him not to damage their newly-cemented alliance by treating Octavia badly. Antony replies tersely that he will be faithful and that Caesar has no cause to be distrustful of him. They say emotional farewells and Antony and Octavia leave.

'But he loves Caesar best, yet he loves Antony:
Hoo! hearts, tongues, figures, scribes, bards, poets, cannot...'

Enobarbus and Agrippa mock the way in which Lepidus plays a political game by professing his exaggerated admiration for the other two triumvirs. Enobarbus is not just criticising Lepidus for his dishonesty, he is acting as a chorus (see page 14) by commenting on the play's action and its recurrent references to the relationship several characters have with their ability to see and tell the truth, or the truth as they would like to have it seen by others.

Enobarbus

'When Antony found Julius Caesar dead,
He cried almost to roaring...'

Antony

Enobarbus criticises Antony for weeping, which undermines his Roman 'manliness' and makes a woman of Antony in the eyes of a soldier. But in Act 4, scene 2, Enobarbus himself is reduced to tears when Antony says his farewells to his associates – although he blames Antony for making him weep.

Act 3 Scene 3

In Alexandria, Cleopatra asks the frightened messenger about Octavia and is pleased at his unflattering descriptions of her. Cleopatra sends the messenger away with gold as a reward.

**'Thou must not take my former sharpness ill,
I will employ thee back again...'**

Here we again meet the unfortunate messenger whom we last saw in Act 2, scene 5 and who, in the interim, has clearly learned a thing or two about the importance of delivering the appropriate news. Whether Octavia conforms to the messenger's description of her, or whether Cleopatra believes him, may not be the point of the scene. Cleopatra wishes the messenger to tell her what she wants to hear because of her feelings for Antony. Whether you see Cleopatra's behaviour as evidence of her arrogant vanity or of her jealousy and need for reassurance will depend on the precise relationship which you feel exists between Antony and Cleopatra. A clue may lie in Charmian's gently supportive comments to her mistress.

This scene also raises the question of how important truthfulness is to the different characters. They continually misread others, their own situation and themselves – whether this is because of ulterior motives or by accident is often difficult to know. Consider, for example, whether it is the case that: Antony and Enobarbus continually over-exaggerate the beauty of Cleopatra; Caesar overestimates Antony's military and political decline; Antony undervalues his own abilities and military strength; Cleopatra does not recognise the stress Antony is under as a result of his feelings about himself and for her.

Act 3 Scene 4

A furious Antony talks to Octavia in Athens and tells her of the news he has heard about Caesar: how he fights new wars against Pompey, has made a will in which Antony hardly features and speaks good things of him with such ill-grace that in reality everyone must know he despises Antony. Octavia tells Antony not to take such news too seriously and offers to mediate between them, an offer which Antony accepts, although meanwhile he will prepare for war between himself and Caesar.

'Husband win, win brother...'

Order and discipline

Octavia is torn between her feelings and loyalties for her brother and her husband. Typically, Antony encourages her to examine her feelings to discover where the greater fault lies, in him or in her brother. When Antony is talking to his wife, do you sense that he is resentful, or compassionate? Octavia is peace-loving and dutiful and contrasts with both the sensual Cleopatra and the cynical Caesar.

**'...if I lose mine honour,
I lose myself.'**

Octavia

Antony speaks to Octavia in typically 'Roman' terms about his need for honour. Ironically, it is exactly because he rejects an entirely Roman conception of self that he is lost to Octavia, although she feels as torn as he does, for similar reasons.

**'Wars 'twixt you twain would be
As if the world should cleave, and that slain men
Should solder up the rift.'**

The world

Octavia stresses the political destruction which would be brought about by war between Caesar and Antony, emphasising the might and power of the two men and echoing the wrenching which she feels within her emotions. Octavia's vision of the ground torn apart and filled with the bodies of the dead is a vision of the future which is soon to come.

Act 3 Scene 5

Eros tells Enobarbus the news about Caesar fighting new wars on Pompey. Caesar and Lepidus have been victorious and Pompey is dead, but Lepidus has been imprisoned and sentenced to death by Caesar, accused of conspiring with Pompey. Eros says Antony is furious that one of his officers should have been used to murder Pompey.

'Caesar and Lepidus have made wars on Pompey.'

Treachery breaks out between the triumvirs, notably on Caesar's side. As the character who most desires earthly power and conquest, Caesar is shown as ruthless and without morals: he attacks Pompey in spite of their peace treaty, then refuses to acknowledge Lepidus's part in the victory but instead throws him into prison under sentence of death. Notice how it was Caesar's refusal to acknowledge the contributions of others which most angered Antony in the previous scene.

Caesar

**'Then, world, thou hast a pair of chaps, no more,
And throw between them all the food thou hast,
They'll grind the one the other.'**

The world

Enobarbus stresses how the two 'chaps' (jaws) of Antony and Caesar will devour the world between them. This image of all things desirable being food and the warriors as consumers of it occurs several times in the play, as when Antony refers to Cleopatra as a 'morsel'. It is the quest for earthly power which is repeatedly shown as the great destroyer of all.

Act 3 Scene 6

In Rome, Caesar complains angrily about the behaviour of Antony, who has taken part in a public ceremony in Egypt with Cleopatra in which they have been crowned as monarchs of the eastern parts of the Roman empire, which Antony has given to her and her children. Caesar says this betrayal is an act of war against Rome. Octavia arrives to mediate between her husband and her brother and Caesar is angry that she has come without any of the ceremony which he feels he should have provided for her. Caesar tells Octavia that he thinks Antony agreed to her coming so that he could be with Cleopatra again. Caesar, Agrippa and Maecenas offer Octavia their sympathy for Antony's adultery.

'Contemning Rome he has done all this, and more, In Alexandria...'

Order and discipline

Caesar is angry that Antony has enthroned Cleopatra as ruler of part of the Roman Empire, although a few lines further on we see him juggling 'fairness' to suit his own purposes so that he may command a share in the wealth and kingdoms of Lepidus. Is Caesar being unfair here, or merely demanding his just share of the conquests?

'Why have you stol'n upon us thus? You come not Like Caesar's sister.'

Only when she arrives in Rome does Octavia learn that Antony has deserted her and returned to Cleopatra. Once Antony's desertion is established in this scene, Octavia vanishes from the play. Caesar's affection for his sister here seems genuine enough and his sympathy for her situation sincere. This contradicts our impressions, both earlier and later in the play, that Caesar is a cold and calculating character with little time for emotion of any kind, let alone warm affection.

Octavia

Shifts in our perspective about characters occur frequently in the play, making us continually review our impressions of them and re-examine their apparent motives; this is especially true of Antony and Cleopatra. This dramatic device is applied through the many scenes in the play and the way they flow on from each other, frequently offering a new view of a situation or character or completely contradicting what has gone before. A good example of this occurs here, where Caesar's injured feelings about the way Antony has been behaving are contrasted with the previous scene, in which Enobarbus and Eros discussed Caesar's betrayal and murder of the triumvirs and allies Lepidus and Pompey. Shakespeare thus encourages the audience to examine and judge characters and motives from several different points of view.

Caesar

Act 3 Scene 7

Near Actium, in Antony's camp, Enobarbus tells Cleopatra that she is an unwelcome distraction to Antony while he is trying to fight the war. Cleopatra refuses to leave. Antony arrives and as he describes how Caesar has made rapid progress, Cleopatra reprimands him for his carelessness. Cleopatra supports Antony in his decision to fight Caesar's army at sea, although Enobarbus and his other military advisers warn him against this as they know they are strongest on land.

'Your presence needs must puzzle Antony...'

Enobarbus offers Cleopatra sound military advice here; her presence will deflect Antony's attention from the business in hand. Also, he tells her, back in Rome there is much critical talk about Antony's decline: the rumour is that Cleopatra's eunuchs and ladies-in-waiting are actually running the war. Cleopatra's reply, that she is president of her kingdom and 'will appear there for a man', emphasises her strength of will, which – some critics have argued – is the ultimate cause of the disaster which befalls the lovers. Antony is swayed by Cleopatra – against the strong advice of his military council and close friends – to continually fight battles at sea, where he is weakest and where he always loses.

'O noble emperor, do not fight by sea,
Trust not to rotten planks.'

The soldier's advice to Antony follows hard upon that of his closest aide, Enobarbus, who has just reminded him of many technical deficiencies in their fighting force if it is to be committed to a sea battle. But Canidius is right in thinking 'we are women's men' and that Antony's judgement will be swayed by the wishes of Cleopatra. The soldier's advice is, in addition, a metaphor for the impermanence of worldly power.

Act 3 Scenes 8 to 10

Three very short scenes in which Caesar tells his general not to commit his land forces until the sea battle is over and Antony instructs Enobarbus to set his soldiers on a hillside where they can see the battle. During the battle Cleopatra's ship flees and is followed by that of Antony, as a result of which the sea battle is lost when otherwise it would have been won. Canidius says he will surrender his army to Caesar, as six kings have already done, but Enobarbus says he will continue to follow Antony, even though his reason argues against it.

'...we have kiss'd away
Kingdoms, and provinces.'

Scarus recognises that Antony's passion for Cleopatra has cost them the battle.

He calls Cleopatra a 'nag' and a 'cow' and rails at her 'magic' which has so corrupted the judgement of Antony.

'I never saw an action of such shame;
Experience, manhood, honour, ne'er before
Did violate so itself.'

Antony

Not for the first time, we see Antony through the eyes of another character; this time Scarus, who comments on his loss of reason and control. Throughout the play we see Antony characterised as one unable to control his excesses, in contrast to Caesar.

Act 3 Scene 11

In Alexandra, Antony feels disgraced by his behaviour in the sea battle and tells his followers that they should leave him. He gives them his ship full of treasure to share between them. Cleopatra enters and says she did not think Antony would follow her ship, but he replies that she knew he would. He has forsaken his power over half the world and will now have to beg terms of peace from Caesar. He has already sent the teacher of their children to Caesar. Cleopatra is apologetic, but Antony tells her to kiss him and that her love is worth all his sacrifice.

'I have fled myself, and have instructed cowards
To run, and show their shoulders.'

Order and discipline

Antony's despair at his failure as a soldier is mingled with the realisation that in more ways than one he has 'fled' himself. The forces which now rule his life are more complex than those which drive the Roman tradition of order and discipline.

'O my lord, my lord,
Forgive my fearful sails! I little thought
You would have follow'd.'

After the battle at Actium, Cleopatra confesses her poor judgement. It seems that she has not, until now, understood the extent to which Antony is under her influence. Antony has lost everything, even his reputation and nobility. If Cleopatra had only her own interests at heart it would be easy at this point for her to abandon Antony. She does not, however, and their love grows noticeably stronger from now on.

Cleopatra

Act 3 Scene 12

At Caesar's camp in Egypt the schoolteacher ambassador from Antony arrives. Dolabella remarks that Antony is fallen indeed, for a few months ago he would have sent one of the kings who served him as a messenger instead. In reply to the ambassador's pleas on behalf of Antony and Cleopatra, Caesar says that Cleopatra may be allowed to keep her throne for her children if she will drive Antony from Egypt or kill him. Caesar then sends Thidias to try to win Cleopatra over to his side and to spy on how Antony is conducting himself in defeat.

'To let him breathe between the heavens and earth, A private man in Athens...'

Antony is indeed between heaven and earth; he is divided between his earthly loyalties and soldierly pursuits and the life of the imagination as represented by his love for Cleopatra. Whilst he is for the moment content to sue for his freedom as a 'private' man, Cleopatra, who has yet to be transformed by her love for Antony, begs instead for kingdoms and the preservation of her worldly power.

Antony

Act 3 Scene 13

Cleopatra asks Enobarbus whether it is she or Antony who is to blame for their present predicament. He tells her the blame is entirely Antony's for allowing his passion to overrule his better judgement. Antony arrives with the ambassador, who has returned with Caesar's reply. Antony says he will meet Caesar in hand-to-hand combat. Enobarbus sees this as a foolish suggestion to which Caesar, sensibly, will never agree, and he wonders whether he is being unwise in continuing to follow Antony. Thidias arrives and Cleopatra tells him that she is willing to surrender to Caesar. As Thidias kisses her hand and commends her on a sensible decision, Antony arrives and becomes angry at this familiarity, ordering Thidias to be taken away and whipped. Antony is furious with Cleopatra for behaving with such unseemly intimacy with an underling. Thidias is sent back to Caesar with the message that Caesar has made Antony angry. Antony forgives Cleopatra when she tells him she still loves him, and says he will fight the war with Caesar. Enobarbus decides that Antony's judgement has become fatally flawed and says he will now leave his master.

'What shall we do, Enobarbus?'

Cleopatra seems to identify her fate wholly with that of Antony by the use of the royal 'we'. Her past confidence is being dissolved by her recognition that Antony's judgement is powerfully swayed by her: 'Is Antony, or we, in fault for this?' she asks. Earlier she was sure of what she was doing in her manipulative games with Antony, but now she is not, as she sees their world unravelling as they sit in her palace with defeat all around them.

'Your Caesar's father oft...
...Bestow'd his lips on that unworthy place...'

The behaviour of Caesar's messenger Thidias, encouraged by Cleopatra, in kissing her hand enrages Antony and results in Thidias being whipped, as Enobarbus anticipates in his immediate aside. It would be considered wholly improper for a messenger to kiss the hand of a royal queen, so the behaviour of Cleopatra angers Antony because it suggests something very unflattering about her. The audience have also just been witness to the invitation by Thidias for Cleopatra to abandon Antony, and so may find Antony's anger well aimed, if ill-informed. Is Cleopatra simply toying with Caesar's messenger and amusing herself like a common whore with her sexual attractiveness; is she signalling her interest in Caesar's offer and suggesting her compliance; or by doing both of these is she hoping to buy some time for her and Antony and trick Caesar?

Cleopatra

'Ah, dear, if I be so,
From my cold heart let heaven engender hail,
And poison it in the source...'

The world

Cleopatra denies that she is cold-hearted towards Antony, as he suggests. The imagery she uses ranges across nature's realm, from the smallest 'gnats of Nile' to the storms of heaven and identifies her capacity for human feeling with the whole of nature. Many of Cleopatra's images are from nature, underlining the universal setting of the plight of the lovers.

'Now he'll outstare the lightning; to be furious
Is to be frightened out of fear...'

Enobarbus is unconvinced by Antony's bold declaration about his renewed spirit for battle, which contrasts with Cleopatra's more measured responses after their greatest quarrel. Antony calls for celebrations to mark what he sees as their turning fortunes and his renewed determination. As he defies death and promises to 'appear in blood' to her, Cleopatra mentions that it is her birthday. Antony remarks with dramatic irony that he will make death love him, for he intends to fight even with death. These references to birth, new beginnings, death and final endings underline fate's role in the action. Enobarbus decides that he must leave Antony, because Antony's renewed valour is foolish in the face of his enemy. Enobarbus feels the accuracy of Antony's military judgement has been deflected once again by his heart.

Enobarbus

Self-test Questions Act 3

Uncover the plot

Delete two of the three alternatives given, to find the correct plot. Beware possible misconceptions and muddles.

Venditius/Canidius/Demetrius warns Seleucus/Gallus/Silius of the dangers of too much military success. Antony and Octavia prepare to leave Egypt/Greece/Rome for Rome/Greece/Egypt. Cleopatra is pleased at what she learns about Antony/Caesar/Octavia because it is amusing/unflattering/useful.

Antony tells Octavia/Cleopatra/Varrius he is angry because Caesar fights/collaborates/argues with Pompey, has left him out of his plans/battles/will and does not think well/often/considerately of him. Octavia says he should be amused by/not ignore/worry about such news. We learn that Mardian/Agrippa/Pompey is dead and that Lepidus/Tarus/Canidius has been sentenced to death/prison/exile for collaborating with him. When Antony learns that one of his officers murdered Pompey he is frightened/glad/angry. Caesar is angry/amused/scornful when he learns that Antony and Cleopatra have been crowned as monarchs of the eastern parts of the Roman empire. Octavia arrives in Rome/Egypt/Greece from Greece/Egypt/Rome and Caesar is angry that she should come alone/so soon/unannounced. Decretas/Maecenas/Caesar tells Octavia/Cleopatra/Alexas that Antony is an adulterer.

In Antony's camp near Actium, Charmian/Enobarbus/Lepidus tells Cleopatra that she should leave. Antony says he will fight Caesar's army at sea – Cleopatra/Enobarbus/Tarus agrees, Tarus/Enobarbus/Cleopatra does not. During the battle Cleopatra's ship sinks/surrenders/flees as a result of which the sea battle is lost. Canidius/Demetrius/Thidias says he will surrender his army to Caesar. Cleopatra's reaction to the battle is one of amusement/sorrow/anger and Antony says her love is worth all his gold/army/sacrifice. Caesar says that Cleopatra may keep her throne if she will surrender/drive Antony from Egypt/marry him or kill/leave/betray Antony. Enobarbus/Antony/Caesar tells Cleopatra that the blame for their present predicament is hers/Pompey's/Antony's. When Antony sees Caesar's messenger Thidias/Dolabella/Philo kissing the hand of Cleopatra he orders him to be sent away/punished/whipped. Enobarbus decides to betray/kill/leave Antony.

Who? What? Why? When? Where? How?

1. Why does Caesar think Antony is quick to agree to Octavia leaving Egypt?
2. What challenge does Antony throw down to Caesar and how is it answered?
3. What do Antony and Caesar say the other has done to anger them?
4. What happens to Thidias and why?
5. What eight things does Cleopatra learn about Octavia from the messenger who arrives in Scene 3?
6. Who does Antony send to Caesar as a messenger?
7. Who decides to leave the service of Antony, surrender his forces and join Caesar's side?
8. Which characters make fun of which other character's over-enthusiastic adulation of Antony and Caesar?
9. Who does Enobarbus blame for Antony's defeats in battle?
10. What most surprises Antony and his followers about the movements of Caesar's forces?

Who said that?

1 'You take from me a great part of myself.'
2 'A lower place, note well,/May make too great an act.'
3 '...when valour preys on reason,/It eats the sword it fights with.'
4 'I have fled myself, and have instructed cowards/To run, and show their shoulders.'
5 '...if I lose mine honour,/I lose myself.'
6 'It is my birthday.'
7 'But it would warm his spirits/To hear from me you had left Antony.'
8 'You did know how much you were my conqueror.'
9 'O noble emperor, do not fight by sea,/Trust not to rotten planks.'
10 'Make me not offended/In your distrust.'

Open quotes

Identify the scene; complete the phrase; identify the speaker and the character being spoken to.

1 'He lessens his requests, and to thee sues...'
2 'Hark, the land bids me tread no more upon't,/It is ashamed to bear me.'
3 'I have offended reputation,'
4 'The greater cantle of the world is lost/With very ignorance, ...'
5 'Egypt, thou knew'st too well,/My heart was...'
6 'To Caesar I will render/My legions and my horse,'
7 'O my lord, my lord,/Forgive my fearful sails!'
8 'Your ships are not well mann'd,'
9 'For learn this, Silius;/Better to leave undone,'
10 'Fall not a tear, I say, one of them rates...'

Act 4 Scene 1

Outside Alexandria, Caesar is scornful of Antony's challenge and he and Maecenas discuss how Antony's behaviour shows that his judgement is flawed. Caesar says that tomorrow will be the final battle and therefore orders that his army feast.

'I have many other ways to die...'

Caesar

Caesar refuses to be drawn by Antony's personal challenge, laughing at the thought that he should risk his present advantage for a test of personal character. This marks the difference between the two men.

Act 4 Scene 2

In Cleopatra's palace inside Alexandria, Antony learns that Caesar has rejected his offer of single combat. He tells his followers that tonight they should feast, for tomorrow he will fight the battle which he will either win or regain his honour by dying. As Antony says his farewells to his followers, in case he does not see them again, they weep – at which he says he did not mean to sadden them, for he expects to achieve victory.

'Give me thy hand, Thou hast been rightly honest...'

Antony receives the news that Caesar will not fight him in single combat and it seems likely from what has gone before that he is the only one to be surprised at this. Antony seems often to be at odds with his followers in his reaction to events; in response here to Cleopatra's puzzlement Enobarbus says that Antony's farewells to his followers are 'one of those odd tricks which sorrow shoots/Out of the mind'. It may seem strange that Antony has not foreseen the effect his melancholy will have on his followers, for he says he spoke to them to comfort them, and he has to try to redress the balance a little later: 'Ho, ho, ho!/Now the witch take me, if I meant it thus!' Again, only Antony seems surprised at the effect his words have had on those around him. It may be that Enobarbus is wrong in his supposition and that Antony's comments here are simply evidence of his great honesty, or it may be that Pompey was right (in Act 2, scene 1) when he described Antony as a 'libertine in a field of feasts' whose judgement is now flawed because his passion for Cleopatra has left his brain 'fuming'.

Order and discipline

'Haply you shall not see me more, or if, A mangled shadow...'

Moments after this, Antony's spirits seem to rise as he reassures his men that he did not mean to depress them, although they find this difficult to believe. However, Antony's comments are truer than he perhaps knows – if not truer than he fears. Antony will all too soon join the world of 'shadow', his physical form 'mangled' and wounded.

Act 4 Scene 3

A short scene, set at night, in which a group of Antony's soldiers on watch hear strange music which they think is coming from all around and underneath them. They suspect that this is the music of the god Hercules, who is associated with Antony and his good fortune so far, and who is now deserting him.

' 'Tis the god Hercules, whom Antony lov'd, Now leaves him.'

The world

The soldiers fear that the music which they think they hear is the sound of Antony's guardian angel leaving him. This is a prophetic conversation, for shortly afterwards Antony is deserted by Enobarbus, who since Antony became involved with Cleopatra has tried to supply him with the calm head and sound military judgement which he seems to have lost. In this respect Enobarbus represents the only presence on stage of Antony's 'other', Herculean, self from the past.

Enobarbus

Act 4 Scene 4

It is morning and Antony rises and is helped to put on his armour by Cleopatra. Antony is in good heart and greets his soldiers in high spirits, after which they all leave Cleopatra and Charmian for the battle.

'I'll leave thee
Now like a man of steel.'

Antony

Cleopatra has helped to buckle on Antony's armour, but his power is waning and it is significant that his words contain not a metaphor, but a simile – he is but 'like' a man of steel. Cleopatra's unfinished sentences at the end of this scene also lead us to wonder how heavy a heart she has at her lover's gallantry.

Act 4 Scene 5

Antony tells Eros, one of his soldiers, that he wishes he had listened to the advice of his colleagues when they told him to fight on land. Eros says that had he taken the advice at the time he would not now be in the position where his kings have revolted and fled. He also tells Antony that Enobarbus has this morning deserted and joined Caesar's side, but has left all his gold and valuables. Antony is not angry but says the possessions of Enobarbus must be sent to him and he will write him a letter saying that he hopes he never has cause to change a master again.

'O, my fortunes have
Corrupted honest men!'

Instead of blaming Enobarbus, Antony blames himself. Note the contrast between this response and the way Caesar treats those who desert Antony.

Act 4 Scene 6

Caesar tells Agrippa to ensure that those who have deserted Antony are placed in the front ranks so that they will be the first to die in the coming battle. Left alone, Enobarbus says many of those who deserted, including himself, have done badly by it or been killed by Caesar. A messenger arrives to tell Enobarbus that all his treasure has arrived from Antony, together with more as a gift. Enobarbus is stricken by conscience and realises that Antony is a better master; he will not fight Antony, but will instead go and find some ditch to die in.

'The time of universal peace is near...'

Order and discipline

Caesar here speaks about his own military victory, but Shakespeare's audience would have also recognised this as a reference to the coming of the Christian Messiah who, significantly when we consider the fate of Antony and Cleopatra, came to teach that worldly wealth and power are less than spiritual salvation.

Act 4 Scene 7

Agrippa and his army retreat before Antony's forces, and although Antony's friend Scarus is wounded, he insists on continuing the fight.

Act 4 Scene 8

Antony praises his soldiers for their victory and allows Scarus Cleopatra's hand to kiss. She says that Scarus shall be given a gold suit of armour which once belonged to a king in reward for his bravery.

'I'll give thee, friend,
An armour all of gold; it was a king's.'

Love and pleasure

Antony offers Scarus Cleopatra's hand to kiss – the same hand which Thidias was whipped for kissing. The armour of gold is a reward and symbolises worldly riches and kingly wealth, in contrast to the practical armour of steel which Antony wore in Scene 5. A celebration is declared, with the wine, music and merriment characteristic of Egyptian excess.

Act 4 Scene 9

Late that night, two sentries witness the dying Enobarbus making a confession to the moon of his guilt in deserting Antony. They watch as he falls to the ground then, as the dawn drums sound, they carry him off.

'Throw my heart
Against the flint and hardness of my fault...'

Under the gaze of the moon, Enobarbus confesses his grief and guilt, then dies. This brief scene serves to reinforce the way the inner spiritual life of humankind cannot be rejected without profound loss. The death of Enobarbus occurs under the starry heavens and is thus associated with the cosmic, heavenly imagery which surrounds the deaths of Antony and Cleopatra. When Antony dies, 'the lamp is out' and light is removed from Cleopatra's world. Antony has sent the treasure of Enobarbus, contrary to the expectations of 'high Roman' values, because of his feelings for him as an individual human being. Enobarbus feels that his own spirit is extinguished because he has turned his back on this essential side of himself.

Act 4 Scenes 10 to 13

Antony tells Scarus that Caesar's forces are preparing to fight at sea, but we discover that Caesar is keeping his best forces on land. Alone, Scarus worries that Cleopatra's soothsayers look grim and dare not speak and, when Antony comes in, he learns that their fleet has surrendered to that of Caesar and that Antony blames Cleopatra for everything. Antony orders Scarus to tell all his men to retreat. Cleopatra enters and Antony angrily tells her to leave him before he gives her what she deserves. He says Caesar will show her off like a captive animal and Octavia will scratch her face with her nails. As Cleopatra leaves, Antony says he will kill her and follows her. Cleopatra takes the advice of Charmian, who tells her to lock herself in the monument for safety and send word to Antony that she has committed suicide.

'All is lost:
This foul Egyptian hath betrayed me...'

Antony rages in fury at what he sees as Cleopatra's deliberate betrayal. His swings of mood with his fortune seem as extreme as those of Cleopatra. In Scene 8 he was praising her as his 'nightingale' after his victory in battle; now he calls her a 'triple-turn'd whore', in reference to her previous alliances with Julius Caesar and then Pompey, and now her presumed turning from him towards Octavius Caesar. It is Antony's lack of control over his passions which here frightens Cleopatra so much that she flees to her monument and sends the fatal message that she has killed herself, thus bringing about the final tragedy. Cleopatra's final ploy, like her earlier ones, is designed to exert control over Antony but she goes too far (as usual?) and provokes a result from which no recovery can be made. Again we see at work the complex dramatic use of the interplay between what different characters mean by, or take to be, the truth.

Antony

Notice also how the structure of the play, with its many short scenes, serves to switch attention rapidly from one perspective to another and from one location to another. These brief and pointed snapshots eventually give way to the final scenes in Cleopatra's monument. The tensions between Rome and Egypt are developed through this structure, with Antony torn between the two. Because of its structure the play possesses a relentless, hurrying feel, with incidents and characters appearing in quick succession in its 42 scenes. This gives the drama a sweeping momentum, which is highly effective, but which not all critics have admired in the past. Only *Hamlet* exceeds *Antony and Cleopatra* in textual length and performing time, although such is the pressure of the action that its length is rarely noticed in the theatre when the play is performed in full.

Order and discipline

Act 4 Scene 14

Antony tells Eros that he has fought the wars for Egypt because he loved Cleopatra and thought she loved him, but that she has betrayed him. As Antony contemplates suicide, Cleopatra's messenger arrives with the news that she has taken her own life.

Antony, in despair that events have come to this, asks Eros to kill him honourably to save his shame. Eros draws his sword as if to kill Antony, but takes his own life instead. In an attempt to kill himself, Antony falls on his sword, but survives, and soldiers who enter refuse to complete his death for him and leave. Diomedes arrives with a message from Cleopatra, saying that she has worried how the news of her suicide might affect Antony and wishes him to know the truth of her whereabouts. Antony's guards are called to carry him to Cleopatra.

'I made these wars for Egypt, and the queen, Whose heart I thought I had, for she had mine...'

After the previous scene, in which Antony and Cleopatra clash angrily, he feels desolate, formless like a cloud, without physical form and substance. This underlines the extent to which Antony feels that his individuality, even his existence, is defined in terms of Cleopatra's love for him.

Antony

Although it was common for battles to be offstage in Shakespeare's works, we see that their reporting in the action of this play is not heavily emphasised. This adds weight to the only two violent events the audience witness, which are the deaths of Antony and Cleopatra. This has the effect of heightening the audience's awareness of the tensions and passions of their love affair, as here, and of concentrating our sympathies on their eventual fate.

'I will o'ertake thee, Cleopatra, and Weep for my pardon.'

Antony is misled into thinking that Cleopatra is dead. In this soliloquy he reveals the extent to which their love has been his only motivating force. In the action of the play love acts as a revelation of the creative life force and a powerful inducement to self-destruction. Despite the quarrels and mistrustfulness, the love between Antony and Cleopatra is an affirmation of the pleasure of existence. Here, however, Antony is driven towards death by the thought of being deprived of his love. In the same way we see that the military might of Rome can be a power for good – in the stability and peace which it can bring – or a force for evil and betrayal, in the treachery and unfeeling inhumanity which it provokes within individuals.

Love and pleasure

'Since Cleopatra died, I have liv'd in such dishonour that the gods Detest my baseness.'

Military conquest, with its recurrent symbol the sword, is associated with visions of great cities and empires, mythological references and the powers

The world

Order and discipline

of nature to emphasise the colossus-like stature of Antony and his impact on the mortal world. Antony recognises that his earthly power has given him many of the attributes of a god: in his time he has 'with my sword/Quartered the world, and o'er green Neptune's back/With ships made cities'. Yet he feels dishonoured and 'base' because he thinks that Cleopatra has died for love of him; he is now 'no more a soldier'. Although tragically mistaken, Antony decides to end his life rather than be taken prisoner into all that remains for him: 'disgrace and horror'. Death 'after the high Roman fashion', as Cleopatra later calls it, belongs to the Roman tradition of stoicism and soldierly dedication, but also owes its appeal here to the bond of personal honour, loyalty, love and sacrifice which Antony and Cleopatra have between them.

'But I will be A bridegroom in my death...'

Anticipating the behaviour of Cleopatra, Antony enters 'the house of death', as he thinks, in pursuit of his love. The image of death as a lover, claiming his victim in marriage, is a familiar one in Shakespeare – it is very prominent in *Romeo and Juliet*, for example – and along with many other romantic or 'spiritual' images is used by both Antony and Cleopatra, in contrast to the more 'concrete' language used by Caesar towards the end of the play.

Act 4 Scene 15

Antony is brought to the monument and is lifted up into it beside Cleopatra. He cautions her to trust none of Caesar's companions but Proculeius, then dies. Cleopatra faints and, when she recovers, announces that after Antony is buried, she will take her own life.

'O sun, Burn the great sphere thou mov'st in, darkling stand The varying shore o' the world.'

The world

As the play progresses, Cleopatra increasingly identifies Antony with heavenly or cosmic forces as a metaphor for the diversity and richness of their relationship and of its universal, timeless setting in the realm of the heavens. This reinforces the universal setting of the action of the play.

'Not Caesar's valour hath o'erthrown Antony, But Antony's hath triumph'd on itself.'

On a purely physical level, Antony is drawn up into the monument, rather than Cleopatra coming down to him, because she fears capture. But this

action is also a visual metaphor, happening in front of the eyes of the audience, for the spiritual elevation of Antony through love. He is lifted up to the heavens into a universe he described in the previous scene, 'where souls do couch on flowers'. In this sense his love has enabled his spirit to triumph over his mortal self and this is indeed 'a heavy sight.'

'O, wither'd is the garland of the war, The soldier's pole is fall'n...'

Cleopatra grieves over the body of Antony, but her words refer not only to the fallen standard (pole) of the conquering soldier but also to worldly power, which is soon 'wither'd'. Only the world of nature and the spirit retains eternal power. The contrast in the imagery of the play between the mortal world and the world of passion and imagination serves to underline the difference between the values of characters such as Caesar and the lovers, and between Rome and Egypt.

Love and pleasure

'Let's do it after the high Roman fashion...'

Cleopatra vows to follow Antony and kill herself as he did: 'a Roman, by a Roman/valiantly vanquish'd'. Earlier, in Act 1, scene 2, she commented critically on the sobering effects on Antony's humour of 'a Roman thought', but in the pursuit of her love she is now keen to embrace the code of conduct which demands that, like Antony, she allows no one to claim victory over her but herself. In many ways we might agree that Antony vanquished or destroyed himself, but Cleopatra's final sacrifice seems to owe its origin more to genuine love than to the call of military honour.

Self-test Questions Act 4

Uncover the plot

Delete two of the three alternatives given, to find the correct plot. Beware possible misconceptions and muddles.

Outside Alexandria/Actium/Athens, Caesar and Thidias/Agrippa/Maecenas are worried/confident/unconcerned about the coming battle against Antony. Antony's soldiers hear screams/earthquakes/strange music at night and think this is a good/puzzling/bad omen. In the morning Antony says he should have taken/ignored/considered the advice to fight the previous battle at sea/in the desert/on land, and learns that Enobarbus/Demetrius/Venditius has run away/deserted/been captured. Antony says the possessions of Enobarbus must be sent to Alexandria/to Rome/after him. Caesar puts those who have deserted Antony at the front/next to him/on a hill in the battle. When Enobarbus hears that his treasure has arrived he is upset/happy/grateful and realises that Antony is a fool/

poor leader/better master than Caesar. Antony's forces win/retreat from/lose the first battle. Seleucus/Scarus/Silius is allowed to kiss the hand of Caesar/Cleopatra/Antony and is given a gold suit of armour for his victory/cleverness/bravery. That night Enobarbus dies through guilt/poison/suicide. The next battle is fought in the mountains/at sea/in Syria: Antony's forces surrender/are defeated/run away, and he blames Cleopatra. Cleopatra hides in the palace/monument/desert and sends a message to Antony that she has committed suicide/left him/take sides with Caesar. Antony asks Eros/Tarus/Varrius to kill him, but he takes his own life/refuses/ignores him. Antony fatally wounds himself with his sword/dagger/spear. Seleucus/Mardian/Diomedes brings a message that Cleopatra is alive. Antony is taken to Cleopatra at the palace/camp/monument and tells her she should trust only Proculeius/Menecrates/Maecenas, then dies. Cleopatra says she will now take her own life/surrender to Caesar/flee to the south.

Who? What? Why? When? Where? How?

1. What is Scarus permitted that other men have been whipped for?
2. What does Antony say that Octavia will do to Cleopatra, if given the chance?
3. Which character kills himself, rather than harm the one he loves?
4. Who acquires a wound which is like an H and whom does he serve?
5. Who calls whom 'the young Roman boy'?
6. What do the soldiers who are on watch think is signified by the music that they hear?
7. Why will Cleopatra not leave her monument, even for the dying Antony?
8. Which characters does Antony ask to help him die, and which ones do so?
9. What does Antony mean when he says that his 'fortunes have corrupted honest men'?
10. Which character is 'valiantly vanquish'd' by a Roman?

Who said that?

1. 'I'll leave thee/Now, like a man of steel.'
2. 'I am alone the villain of the earth.'
3. 'We have beat them to their beds.'
4. 'None about Caesar trust but Proculeius.'
5. 'Farewell, great chief. Shall I strike now?'
6. '...the long day's task is done,/And we must sleep.'
7. 'Thou art/The armourer of my heart.'
8. 'Triple-turn'd whore.'
9. 'Retire, we have engag'd ourselves too far.'
10. 'The time of universal peace is near.'

Open quotes

Identify the scene; complete the phrase; identify the speaker and the character being spoken to.

1. 'O, wither'd is the garland of the war,/The soldier's pole is fall'n: young boys and girls...' (Complete next three lines.)
2. 'Throw my heart/Against the flint and hardness of my fault,'
3. 'O sun, thy uprise shall I see no more,'
4. 'But I will be/A bridegroom in my death,'
5. 'Since Cleopatra died,/I have liv'd...'
6. 'Not Caesar's valour hath o'erthrown Antony,'
7. 'Caesar must think,/When one so great begins to rage,'
8. 'Perchance to-morrow/You'll serve another master.'
9. 'Caesar to Antony: let the old ruffian know'
10. 'By sea and land I'll fight: or I will live,'

Act 5 Scene 1

Caesar sends Dolabella to demand Antony's surrender, but Decretas appears at Caesar's camp with Antony's sword and reports that his master is dead by his own hand. Caesar and his followers are saddened at this news. An Egyptian messenger arrives from Cleopatra asking what Caesar intends to do, so that Cleopatra may decide the course of action she should take. Caesar tells the messenger that he intends no harm to Cleopatra. As the messenger leaves, Caesar tells Proculeius to follow and observe Cleopatra to make sure she does not commit suicide, for her appearance in Rome will confirm Caesar's triumph for ever.

'The breaking of so great a thing should make A greater crack...'

Antony

Cleopatra

Decretas appears holding the sword of Antony, all that is left of him in the world of mortals. This powerful visual image is the culmination of a subtle train of metaphor which runs throughout the play, the sword as a symbol of military might and sexual potency. In Act 2 Agrippa commented that Cleopatra once 'made great Caesar lay his sword to bed./He ploughed her and she cropped'. The imagery skilfully mingles ideas of military and sexual conquest, although we should note that in Agrippa's account it was Cleopatra who vanquished Caesar sexually. The notion of Cleopatra as a great victor of men by virtue of her sensuousness and lust is repeated often; she dresses the drunken Antony in her clothes then wears his sword herself; Antony derides Caesar in Act 3 for wearing his sword 'e'en like a dancer' and challenges him to single combat 'sword against sword' as a way to define who is the true victor between them. When things go badly for Antony and he knows he will have to beg to Caesar for mercy, he tells Cleopatra: 'You did know/How much you were my conqueror, and that/ My sword, made weak by my affection, would/Obey it on all cause.' By Act 4, scene 14, he cries: 'She has robb'd me of my sword'.

'Go and say We purpose her no shame...'

Caesar

Caesar has no scruples when it comes to achieving his military objectives. This makes him a powerful warrior, but contrasts his code of military values with those of Antony and of Cleopatra, who sees through his lies in any case.

Act 5 Scene 2

In the monument, Cleopatra announces that she is now content to die. Proculeius arrives, to tell her that Caesar will grant her whatever she wishes. Cleopatra says that Antony assured her of Proculeius's trustworthiness, and says that she wishes her son to be given Egypt. Proculeius tells her she will find Caesar generous. Suddenly, Caesar's soldiers appear, having secretly gained entry to the monument to capture Cleopatra. She tries to kill herself with a dagger, but is disarmed by Proculeius, who then leaves to take her message to Caesar. Dolabella is left in charge and Cleopatra says she wishes to sleep, so that she might dream of another man as mighty as Antony. Moved by her description of Antony, Dolabella admits to Cleopatra that Caesar intends to parade her in the streets in Rome.

Caesar enters and tells Cleopatra that he will put her children to death if she tries to kill herself. She gives Caesar a list of all her possessions but her treasurer, Seleucus, says the list is incomplete. Although Cleopatra is furious at this, Caesar tells her it does not matter, for she may keep anything she wishes. After Caesar leaves, Cleopatra sends Charmian on a secret errand, convinced now that Caesar will parade her in Rome for the common people to stare at. Dolabella arrives to tell Cleopatra that Caesar intends her to leave for Rome in three days. The guard brings Cleopatra some figs, then a clown, whom Cleopatra orders to stay when the guard leaves. The clown has secretly brought asps (poisonous snakes) in a basket. Cleopatra dresses in her robe, crown and jewels; she kisses Charmian and Iras, who falls and dies. Cleopatra puts an asp to her breast and one to her arm and dies, longing to be reunited with Antony. As the guard enters, Charmian kills herself with an asp. Caesar returns and declares that Cleopatra shall be buried in state with Antony.

' 'Tis paltry to be Caesar: Not being Fortune, he's but Fortune's knave, A minister of her will...'

Cleopatra sees herself as about to be released from the shackles of the physical world as she contemplates her own death. We learn little of how Caesar, the archetypal Roman, feels about things; he remains a private man who suppresses his tears even at the parting with his own sister. Although Cleopatra understands that Antony owes something of himself to the traditional Roman values of order and discipline, she knows that he is more than this: a mixture of discipline and passion. Caesar represents a power which, because it is one-dimensional, is essentially inhuman, sterile and unfulfilling.

Order and discipline

'His face was as the heavens...'

For Cleopatra, Antony has now truly become a god, whose arm can encircle the world and whose legs bestride the oceans. He is a creature 'past the size of dreaming', 'an emperor Antony', who need have no fear of being eclipsed by Caesar. Later Cleopatra's 'immortal longings' draw her to his side. By her death, she has defeated Caesar.

The world

**'...'tis exactly valued,
Not petty things admitted.'**

The incident with Seleucus involving Cleopatra and her possessions has puzzled many critics. Cleopatra's servants have so far been characterised by fierce loyalty, so in contradicting Cleopatra – publicly calling her a liar, in effect – Seleucus goes against this pattern, but no real reason is given to explain this. Some argue that Cleopatra has simply been caught out at last, and this demonstrates how fickle and capricious she is – she clearly planned to survive at whatever cost. Others feel that she is here being her usual clever and manipulative self – by pretending to lie about her precious possessions, she might trick Caesar into believing that she has no intention of taking her own life. If she can convince him that she is more concerned to hoard treasure for the future than anything else, he may be caught sufficiently off guard for her to succeed in her suicide.

Cleopatra

**'He words me, girls, he words me, that I should not
Be noble to myself...'**

Although Cleopatra is driven by her passions to a far greater extent than Caesar seems to be, she is shrewd and observant and sees through his false reassurances at once. This is a meeting between a young and calculating Caesar, who is in a very strong position, and a more seasoned politician who is aware of the disadvantages and opportunities of her much weaker situation. As Antony remarked near the start of the play (Act 1, scene 2), Cleopatra is 'cunning past man's thought'.

**'...and I shall see
Some squeaking Cleopatra boy my greatness
I' the posture of a whore.'**

Occasional offence was taken in Shakespeare's time by the then customary practice of having boys play the female roles on stage. Cleopatra's remark here is therefore both an interesting contemporary comment on the times and an emphasis of her determination not to be humbled. Like Antony, Cleopatra has a Roman soldier's sense of honour.

**'I have nothing
Of woman in me: now from head to foot
I am marble-constant...'**

Love and pleasure

Throughout the play Cleopatra's femininity has – as she admits – been characterised by inconstency or, as Enobarbus put it, her 'infinite variety'. Now her need to manipulate is past and we see her forsake the assumed 'womanly' side of her character. Looking back at the incidents involving Cleopatra, we can speculate on the extent to which she has used the typical courtesan's behaviour in assuming false emotions when it suited her. Some critics have seen Cleopatra's behaviour, and even her death, as typical of a persistent theatricality in her character.

'You must not think I am so simple but I know the devil himself will not eat a woman...'

It might at first glance seem strange that it should be a clown who brings in the asps, but throughout the play, humour has been used skilfully to lighten the tone and provide illuminating contrasts with the previous action as well as preparation for that which is to come. Although the outcome of the play is tragedy, it also has features of a comedy, notably in its overall structure. Egypt and Rome perform similar functions to the court and the forest in *A Midsummer Night's Dream*: worlds set apart within other worlds, in which characters explore different realities. *Antony and Cleopatra* is also on many occasions a very funny play: Cleopatra's teasing of Antony at the start of the action; her references to dressing him in her clothes whilst he is drunk; the bawdy jibes of her courtiers (Act 1, scene 2); and her robust treatment of the luckless messenger. Similarly we see Lepidus as an amusing drunk, with Antony studiously playing the fool about the appearance of a crocodile; and Enobarbus and Agrippa scoff at Lepidus's praises of Caesar and Antony. This humorous element of the play vanishes after Act 3, scene 3, when the fragile peace between the triumvirs begin to fall apart, until its reappearance here. This mixing of politics, love, victory and defeat is set within the quite complex structure of the play; a structure which owes something to Shakespeare's tragedies and also his romantic comedies. In some ways *Antony and Cleopatra* anticipates his later romances, in which the magical transfiguration of humanity is explored.

'I am fire, and air; my other elements I give to baser life.'

Cleopatra takes her leave of her ladies-in-waiting, crying that she goes to join her husband in obedience to her 'immortal longings'. She welcomes death because her love for Antony – whom she now sees as a god-like being – has transformed her from an earthly creature into 'fire, and air'. These elements fittingly remind us of Cleopatra's fiery and changeable temperament and her passionate nature. Their love cannot separate them, and has at last put them beyond the reach of the world's buffeting.

Cleopatra

'Dost thou not see my baby at my breast, That sucks the nurse asleep?'

Throughout the play serpents, snakes, crocodiles and similar creatures have

been used – echoing the serpent in the Garden of Eden – as mysterious creatures of betrayal. Here Cleopatra takes her own life in a typically sensuous act of surrender, such is her willingness to embrace death. As befits one so closely identified with her mistress, Charmian follows her to death, after checking that her queen's royal appearance is as it should be.

'No grave upon the earth shall clip in it A pair so famous.'

Caesar's victory is complete and his military and political control of the physical world serves as one resolution of the action of the play. This outcome is both an affirmation of the potential of Caesar's spirit, as spoken of by the soothsayer, and is at the same time incomplete. The fate of Antony and Cleopatra is a result of the conflicting demands placed upon them by the world of Caesar and yet it transcends that world. The lovers rise above the restrictions and values of the real world. This acts as a second resolution of the action and a metaphor for the 'time of universal peace' which Caesar says he will usher in, except that the peace of the lovers is a spiritual one, not a civil and political one. Shakespeare's audiences would also have seen the lovers' fate as a clear example of the dramatic irony of Caesar's words and the 'universal peace' which will be brought about by the coming of the Messiah.

This last scene of the play is easily the longest and forms an effective contrast with the many previous scenes in having a fixed location inside the monument within which Cleopatra is trapped. The focus in Act 5 narrows onto Cleopatra and concentrates on her spiritual union with Antony. Cleopatra is also physically reunited with Antony in her burial, emphasising Caesar's domination of the mortal world of conquest and power.

Antony and Cleopatra know that love is more destructive than war, more threatening than military might, because a lover's identity is defined in terms of the one who loves them. This may be why the Roman characters feel threatened by the sensual excesses of Egypt, which have drawn many previous generals under their influence.

Self-test Questions Act 5

Uncover the plot

Delete two of the three alternatives given, to find the correct plot. Beware possible misconceptions and muddles.

Caesar sends Dolabella/Menas/Canidius to demand Antony's life/empire/surrender. Demetrius/Scarus/Dercetas appears at Caesar's camp with Antony's sword/treasure/surrender and reports that his master is dead. Caesar and his followers are joyful/saddened/relieved at this news. Proculeius/Caesar/Dolabella tells Caesar/Proculeius/Dolabella to make sure Cleopatra does not escape/hide in her monument/commit suicide. Cleopatra says she is now content to die/marry Caesar/surrender. Caesar/Proculeius/Dolabella says he is sure she will be treated well. Suddenly, Gallus/Scarus/Sextus and soldiers of Caesar appear. Cleopatra tries to kill herself with a sword/snake/dagger. Later, Charmian/Dolabella/Menas reveals that Caesar intends to parade/marry/execute her in Rome. Caesar arrives and says he will kill Cleopatra's servants/parents/children if she does what Antony has done. She gives Caesar an incomplete list of all her forces/jewels/possessions but Seleucus/Mardian/Diomedes betrays her. Cleopatra secretly arranges for Iras/Dolabella/the clown to bring her asps. Cleopatra kisses her attendants/mother/children. Iras/Charmian/Mardian falls and dies. Cleopatra kills herself with cuts/asps/poison to her breast/throat/side and heart/arm/stomach. Iras/Charmian/Mardian takes her life with an asp. Caesar returns with Tarus/Canidius/Dolabella and says Cleopatra shall be buried with her parents/Antony/her children, after which he will go to Athens/Rome/Misenum.

Who? What? Why? When? Where? How?

1 What convinces Caesar that Cleopatra did not die by taking poison?
2 Which character confirms Cleopatra's suspicions about how Caesar intends to treat her in Rome?
3 With what does Caesar threaten Cleopatra if she takes her life?
4 Who goes to arrange for the asps to be brought in and how are these concealed from the guards?
5 According to the clown, how many women do devils mar?
6 Which character says of which other character that their 'taints and honours' were equally matched within them?
7 Cleopatra is stopped from stabbing herself by whom?
8 What reasons does Cleopatra give Caesar for her withholding some of her possessions from the list she gives him?
9 According to Dolabella, how soon does Caesar intend to send Cleopatra to Rome and what route will he take?
10 How do Charmian and Iras die?

Who said that?

1 'It is well done, and fitting for a princess/Descended of so many royal kings.'
2 'I know, that a woman is a dish for the gods, if the devil dress her not.'
3 'He words me, girls, he words me.'
4 'I am fire, and air; my other elements/I give to baser life.'
5 'I am sure my nails/Are stronger than mine eyes.'
6 'A rarer spirit never/Did steer humanity.'
7 'Caesar's no merchant, to make prize with you/Of things that merchants sold.'
8 'Where art thou, death?/Come hither, come...'
9 'This is his sword,/I robb'd his wound of it.'
10 'I have immortal longings in me.'

Open quotes

Identify the scene; complete the phrase; identify the speaker and the character being spoken to.

1 'Peace, peace!/Dost thou not see my baby at my breast,'
2 'Take up her bed,/And bear her women...'
3 'My resolution's plac'd, and I have nothing/Of woman in me'
4 '...thyself art coming/To see perform'd the dreaded act...'
5 'His face was as the heavens, and therein struck/A sun and moon, ...'
6 'Antony/Shall be brought drunken forth, and I shall see/Some squeaking...'
7 'We purpose her no shame: give her what comforts/The quality of her passion shall require,'
8 'Now boast thee, death, in thy possession lies...'
9 'Rather a ditch in Egypt/Be gentle grave unto me, rather on Nilus's mud...'
10 'The breaking of so great a thing...'

Self-test Answers Act 1

Uncover the plot

In Alexandria two friends of Antony's talk about how his involvement with Queen Cleopatra is causing him to ignore his military responsibilities. When news arrives from Rome, Cleopatra taunts Antony that this may be a message from Fulvia or from Caesar. Antony says he will stay in Egypt. A soothsayer foretells the futures of Charmian and Iras. Antony learns that his wife has battled with his brother, after which they have both fought Caesar, who has been victorious. Antony also learns that the Parthians have conquered Roman territory. Another messenger tells him that his wife has died. Antony decides to return to Rome and help Caesar fight Pompey. Cleopatra is resigned about this. Caesar tells Lepidus about Antony's life in Egypt. News arrives that his enemy is now helped by Menecrates and Menas, who are pirates. Cleopatra sends messengers to Antony every day to tell him how much she loves him. Charmian reminds Cleopatra that she once loved Caesar as much years before.

Who? What? Why? When? Where? How?

1. Alexas tells Cleopatra this about the messengers she has sent to Antony (who has gone to Rome) every day since he left
2. Caesar says he has heard that Antony did this whilst crossing the Alps, because there was nothing else available
3. She says, teasingly (tauntingly?), that maybe Fulvia his wife is angry with him, or perhaps the young Caesar has sent orders for him to obey
4. Fishing, drinking, staying up all night revelling (noisy merrymaking), being no more like a man than is Cleopatra and behaving more like a woman than a soldier
5. Cleopatra asks for this from Charmian, so that she might sleep through the time when Antony is away from her
6. Mardian is, says Cleopatra, free of sexual desire (which she is plagued by, because Antony is away in Rome) because he is a eunuch
7. According to Cleopatra, Antony calls her this
8. A strumpet's fool
9. Philo, in Act 1, scene 1
10. That they will be 'far fairer' than they presently are; that they will be more 'beloving' than 'belov'd'; and that they will both outlive Cleopatra

Who said that, and to whom?

1. Iras, talking to Charmian in Act 1, scene 2
2. Antony, talking to the messenger in Act 1, scene 2
3. Caesar, talking to Lepidus in Act 1, scene 4
4. These are the first words of the play, spoken by Philo to Demetrius about Antony
5. Enobarbus, talking to Antony in Act 1, scene 2
6. Charmian, advising Cleopatra about her relationship with Antony in Act 1, scene 3
7. Cleopatra, talking to Charmian in Act 1, scene 5
8. Antony, talking to the messenger in Act 1, scene 2
9. Charmian, talking to Cleopatra about Antony in Act 1, scene 5
10. The second messenger, talking to Antony in Act 1, scene 2

Open quotes

1. 'And wrinkled deep in time.' Cleopatra, talking to Mardian in Act 1, scene 5
2. 'Alack, sir, no, her passions are made of nothing but the finest part of pure love.' Enobarbus in Act 1, scene 2, answering Antony's criticism of Cleopatra's behaviour

3 'Or lose myself in dotage.' Antony, talking to the messengers in Act 1, scene 2
4 'And fertile every wish, a million.' The soothsayer, answering Charmian's question in Act 1, scene 2, about how many children she will have in the future
5 'Ten thousand harms, more than the ills I know,/My idleness doth hatch.' Antony, in a soliloquy in Act 1, scene 2, musing about his entanglement with Cleopatra and the risks he runs because of this
6 '...our dungy earth alike/Feeds beast as man.' Antony, talking to Cleopatra in Act 1, scene 1, about how their love is more important to him than his duty to Caesar, Fulvia, or Rome
7 'Thou teachest like a fool: the way to lose him.' Cleopatra, answering Charmian's warning about her treatment of Antony. Act 1, scene 3
8 '... to the deserver/Till his deserts are past.' Antony, talking to Enobarbus in Act 1, scene 2 about the fickleness of the common people of Rome
9 '... though between them and a great cause, they should be esteemed nothing.' Enobarbus in Act 1, scene 2, talking to Antony about the dangers of his attachment to Cleopatra
10 'How mine receiv'd shall be.' Cleopatra, talking to Antony in Act 1, scene 3

Self-test Answers Act 2

Uncover the plot

Pompey is based in Messina and feels confident about his chances of winning the coming battles. News arrives that Antony is travelling to Rome. Lepidus asks Enobarbus to help him with the meeting between Caesar and Antony. Antony says he had no involvement in the rebellion of his wife and brother. Antony says he did not respond to messages for help because he had a hangover. They agree to unite to fight Pompey. Antony agrees to marry Caesar's sister, Octavia. Enobarbus says Antony will never leave Cleopatra. Although just married, Antony decides his future lies in Alexandria. Caesar and Antony are to meet at Misenum for the campaign against Pompey. Cleopatra hears of the marriage of Antony and is furious at the news. Pompey, Caesar, Lepidus and Antony meet to agree a truce. During a banquet on Pompey's ship Menas suggests to Pompey that they should cut the throats of the others. This plan does not work because it is rejected. The generals enjoy themselves at the feast until Caesar says that this behaviour does not suit their serious business.

Who? What? Why? When? Where? How?

1 Because he carries off a third of the world (as far as military leadership is concerned)
2 The soothsayer
3 She sailed her barge down the river Cydnus whilst Antony sat on a throne in the city marketplace. When she landed Antony accepted her invitation to dine with her aboard her ship
4 Menas tells Pompey this aboard their ship when the other triumvirs are feasting
5 Around Mount Misena
6 A crocodile, according to Antony
7 He tells Menas, at the start of the first scene in Act 2, that Antony is entertaining himself ('sits at dinner') in Egypt, Caesar taxes his people too much for them to follow him ('gets money where he loses hearts'), and although Lepidus flatters and is flattered in return by the other two, he in fact dislikes them (and they him) and so will not join forces against Pompey

8 Antony says that she did it to get him out of Egypt
9 Agrippa suggests that if Antony marries Octavia then she, as Caesar's sister, would act as intermediary between them (eliminating damaging half-truths and rumours) and would unite them as a family by sharing their mutual responsibility and love for her
10 Because Pompey now knows about the deed before it is done, he feels it would dishonour him to agree to it, although he admits that he would have been pleased with Menas if he had done it and then told him about it later

Who said that and about whom?

1 Enobarbus, talking about Antony in Act 2, scene 2
2 Antony, talking to Octavia about his own responsibilities in Act 2, scene 3
3 Lepidus, talking to Enobarbus about Antony in Act 2, scene 2
4 Enobarbus, talking about Cleopatra in Act 2, scene 2
5 Pompey, talking to Antony (possibly with a double meaning) about Caesar and Cleopatra's hospitality in Act 2, scene 6
6 Cleopatra, talking to Charmian about her anger at the news of Antony's marriage in Act 2, scene 5
7 Menecrates, talking to Pompey about their fortunes, in Act 2, scene 1
8 Enobarbus, talking to Menecrates about Antony in Act 2, scene 6
9 The soothsayer, talking to Antony about Caesar in Act 2, scene 3
10 Pompey, talking about himself in Act 2, scene 1

Open quotes

1 '... the operation of your sun: so is your crocodile.' Lepidus, talking to Antony in Act 2, scene 7
2 'I' the east my pleasure lies.' Antony, talking about Cleopatra in a soliloquy at the end of Act 2, scene 3
3 'Shall never find it more.' Menas, in an aside in Act 2, scene 7, after Pompey has rejected his offer to slit the throats of the other triumvirs on the ship
4 'Her infinite variety: other women cloy/The appetites they feed, but she makes hungry,/Where most she satisfies.' Enobarbus, talking to Maecenas and Agrippa about Cleopatra, in Act 2, scene 2
5 '... the very strangler of their amity.' Enobarbus, talking to Menas about Antony's marriage to Octavia in Act 2, scene 6
6 '... to bed;/He plough'd her, and she cropp'd.' Agrippa, talking about Cleopatra to Enobarbus in Act 2, scene 2
7 'Caesar's sister is called Octavia.' Enobarbus replies thus to the question asked by Menas in Act 2, scene 6
8 '... fall to their throats.' Menecrates, talking to Pompey in Act 2, scene 7
9 'strange courtesies and great/Of late upon me: I must thank him only.' Antony, talking to Caesar and Lepidus in Act 2, scene 2
10 '...his soldiership/Is twice the other twain.' Pompey, talking to Varrius and Menecrates about Antony in Act 2, scene 1

Self-test Answers Act 3

Uncover the plot

Venditius warns Silius of the dangers of too much military success. Antony and Octavia prepare to leave Rome for Egypt. Cleopatra is pleased at what she learns about Octavia because it is unflattering.

Antony tells Octavia he is angry because Caesar fights with Pompey, has left him out of his will and does not think well of him. Octavia says he should not worry about such news. We learn that Pompey is dead and that Lepidus has been sentenced to death for collaborating with him. When Antony learns that one of his officers murdered Pompey he is angry. Caesar is angry when he learns that Antony and Cleopatra have been crowned as monarchs of the eastern parts of the Roman empire. Octavia arrives in Rome from Egypt and Caesar is angry that she should come unannounced. Caesar tells Octavia that Antony is an adulterer. In Antony's camp near Actium, Enobarbus tells Cleopatra that she should leave. Antony says he will fight Caesar's army at sea – Cleopatra agrees, Enobarbus does not. During the battle Cleopatra's ship flees as a result of which the sea battle is lost. Canidius says he will surrender his army to Caesar. Cleopatra's reaction to the battle is one of sorrow and Antony says her love is worth all his sacrifice. Caesar says that Cleopatra may keep her throne if she will drive Antony from Egypt or kill Antony. Enobarbus tells Cleopatra that the blame for their present predicament is Antony's. When Antony sees Caesar's messenger Thidias kissing the hand of Cleopatra he orders him to be whipped. Enobarbus decides to leave Antony.

Who? What? Why? When? Where? How?

1 Caesar thinks Antony sees Octavia's continued presence in Egypt as some kind of impediment to his lustful pursuit of Cleopatra
2 Antony challenges Caesar to single-combat as a way of deciding the outcome of their military struggle, but Caesar rejects this
3 Antony says that Caesar has started new wars against Pompey (breaking the truce), and when he has spoken of Antony has done so in a grudging way which made it abundantly clear to all who heard that he thought little of him. For his part Caesar says that Antony has enthroned himself and Cleopatra as monarchs of a large part of the Roman empire, and established his sons as kings of kings
4 Antony has him whipped for being so presumptuous as to kiss the hand of Cleopatra
5 Octavia is not as tall as Cleopatra; she is low-voiced; she has no majesty when she walks; she was a widow; the messenger puts her age at thirty; her face is round; her hair is brown; and she has a low forehead
6 His children's schoolmaster
7 Antony's lieutenant-general, Canidius
8 Agrippa and Enobarbus mock Lepidus (in his absence) for this
9 He blames Antony, who should have known better than to allow his feelings to override his judgement
10 They are most surprised at how swiftly Caesar's forces are moving through territory and gaining victories

Who said that?

1 Caesar, talking to Antony about Octavia in Act 3, scene 2
2 Venditius, talking to Silius about the risks in achieving more than your master in Act 3, scene 1
3 Enobarbus, deciding to leave the service of Antony in Act 3, scene 8
4 Antony, following his defeat in the sea battle in Act 3, scene 11
5 Antony, when explaining to Octavia why he is upset at Caesar's recent treatment of him in Act 3, scene 4
6 Cleopatra in Act 3, scene 13
7 Thidias, talking to Cleopatra in Act 3, scene 13
8 Antony, speaking to Cleopatra in Act 3, scene 11
9 A soldier, advising Antony in Act 3, scene 7

10 Antony, when rebuking Caesar for warning him to take care of Octavia in Act 3, scene 2

Open quotes

1 'To let him breathe between the heavens and earth,/A private man in Athens.' Antony's ambassador (the schoolmaster) speaking to Caesar in Act 3, scene 12, seeking for terms after Antony's defeat

2 'Friends, come hither: I am so lated in the world that I/Have lost my way for ever.' Antony, talking to his attendants in Act 3, scene 11, about his fortunes after his defeat

3 'A most unnoble swerving.' Antony, talking in Act 3, scene 11, to Eros about his defeat

4 '... we have kiss'd away/Kingdoms, and provinces.' Scarus, talking to Enobarbus in Act 3, scene 10 about the way Cleopatra's ship turned away from the battle, was followed by Antony's and their victory was lost

5 '... to thy rudder tied by the strings.' Antony, talking to Cleopatra in Act 3, scene 11, about how he followed her ship when it left the battle

6 '... six kings already/Show me the way of yielding.' Canidius, talking to Scarus and Enobarbus in Act 3, scene 10, about his decision to leave Antony and join Caesar's side

7 'I little thought/You would have follow'd.' Cleopatra, talking to Antony in Act 3, scene 11, about her actions during the sea battle

8 'Your mariners are muleteers, reapers, people/Ingross'd by swift impress.' Enobarbus, talking to Antony in Act 3, scene 7, in an attempt to persuade him not to fight the coming battle at sea

9 'than by our deed/Acquire too high a fame, when him we serve's away.' Venditius, talking to Silius in Act 3, scene 1, about the foolishness of achieving too much

10 'All that is won and lost.' Antony, talking to Cleopatra in Act 3, scene 11, about the price of his defeat

Self-test Answers Act 4

Uncover the plot

Outside Alexandria, Caesar and Maecenas are confident about the coming battle against Antony.

Antony's soldiers hear strange music at night and think this is a bad omen. In the morning Antony says he should have taken the advice to fight the previous battle on land, and learns that Enobarbus has deserted. Antony says the possessions of Enobarbus must be sent after him. Caesar puts those who have deserted Antony at the front in the battle. When Enobarbus hears that his treasure has arrived he is upset and realises that Antony is a better master. Antony's forces win the first battle. Scarus is allowed to kiss the hand of Cleopatra and is given a gold suit of armour for his bravery. That night Enobarbus dies through guilt. The next battle is fought at sea and Antony's forces surrender and he blames Cleopatra. Cleopatra hides in the monument and sends a message to Antony that she has committed suicide. Antony asks Eros to kill him, who takes his own life. Antony wounds himself fatally with his sword. Diomedes brings a message that Cleopatra is alive. Antony is taken to Cleopatra at the monument and tells her she should trust only Proculeius, then dies. Cleopatra says she will now take her own life.

Who? What? Why? When? Where? How?

1 He is allowed to kiss the hand of Cleopatra
2 Scratch her face with her nails
3 Eros
4 Scarus, in the service of Antony
5 Antony directs this scathing comment at Caesar
6 That Antony's protecting god Hercules is deserting him
7 She says that she fears capture by Caesar's soldiers
8 Antony asks five: Eros, two guards, Decretas, Diomedes, none of whom obey him
9 Antony refers to the desertion of Enobarbus, for which he blames himself
10 Antony, who takes his own life rather than have to 'put off my helmet to my countryman'

Who said that?

1 Antony, when saying farewell to Cleopatra before the battle in Act 4, scene 3
2 Enobarbus, on learning that his treasure has arrived after him in Act 4, scene 6
3 Antony, talking about the battle in Act 4, scene 8
4 Antony, advising Cleopatra in Act 4, scene 15
5 Eros, to Antony in Act 4, scene 14
6 Antony, when he hears from Mardian that Cleopatra has killed herself in Act 4, scene 14
7 Antony, to Cleopatra in Act 4, scene 4
8 Antony, talking to Scarus about Cleopatra in Act 4, scene 12
9 Agrippa, talking to his men during the battle in Act 4, scene 7
10 Caesar, talking to his men before the battle in Act 4, scene 6

Open quotes

1 'Are level now with men: the odds is gone,/And there is nothing left remarkable/beneath the visiting moon.' Cleopatra, talking to Charmian and Iras over the body of Antony in Act 4, scene 15
2 'Which being dried with grief, will break to powder,/And finish all foul thoughts.' Enobarbus, when he thinks himself alone in Act 4, scene 9
3 'Fortune and Antony part here, even here/Do we shake hands.' Antony, in a soliloquy in Act 4, scene 12
4 '... and run into't/As to a lover's bed.' Antony, talking to Eros in Act 4, scene 14
5 '... in such dishonour that the gods/Detest my baseness.' Antony, talking to Eros in Act 4, scene 14
6 'But Antony's hath triumph'd on itself.' Antony, talking to Cleopatra in Act 4, scene 15
7 '... he's hunted/Even to falling.' Maecenas, talking to Caesar in Act 4, scene 1, about Antony
8 'I look on you,/As one that takes his leave.' Antony, talking to his followers in Act 4, scene 2
9 'I have many other ways to die; meantime/Laugh at his challenge.' Caesar, talking in Act 4, scene 1, to Maecenas about Antony's challenge to single-combat
10 'Or bathe my dying honour in the blood/Shall make it live again.' Antony, talking to Enobarbus when he learns that Caesar will not fight him in single-combat, in Act 4, scene 2

Self-test Answers Act 5

Uncover the plot

Caesar sends Dolabella to demand Antony's surrender. Dercetas appears at Caesar's camp with Antony's sword and reports that his master is dead. Caesar and his followers are saddened at this news. Caesar tells Proculeius to make sure Cleopatra does not commit suicide. Cleopatra says she is now content to die. Proculeius says he is sure she will be treated well. Suddenly, Gallus and soldiers of Caesar appear. Cleopatra tries to kill herself with a dagger. Later, Dolabella reveals that Caesar intends to parade her in Rome. Caesar arrives and says he will kill Cleopatra's children if she does what Antony has done. She gives Caesar an incomplete list of all her possessions but Seleucus betrays her. Cleopatra secretly arranges for the clown to bring her asps. Cleopatra kisses her attendants. Iras falls and dies. Cleopatra kills herself with asps to her breast and arm. Charmian takes her life with an asp. Caesar returns with Dolabella and says Cleopatra shall be buried with Antony, after which he will go to Rome.

Who? What? Why? When? Where? How?

1 There is no sign of external swelling on her body
2 Dolabella
3 He says he will kill her children
4 Charmian goes to arrange this. The asps are smuggled in concealed in a basket of figs
5 Five out of every ten
6 Maecenas says this of Antony
7 Proculeius
8 As small gifts for her friends; and as nobler gifts for Livia and Octavia in Rome
9 Dolabella says Caesar intends to send Cleopatra and her children ahead of him within three days. He will travel through Syria
10 Charmian dies by allowing an asp to bite her; Iras falls and dies after kissing Cleopatra farewell

Who said that?

1 Charmian, responding to the guard's question about Cleopatra's suicide in Act 5, scene 2
2 The clown, answering Cleopatra's question on whether the asp will eat her in Act 5, scene 2
3 Cleopatra, talking to Iras and Charmian about how she regards Caesar's promises to her in Act 5, scene 2
4 Cleopatra, talking to Charmian and Iras just before she takes her own life in Act 5, scene 2
5 Iras, explaining why she will never see Cleopatra humbled in Rome in Act 5, scene 2
6 Agrippa, on learning of Antony's death in Act 5, scene 1
7 Caesar, reassuring Cleopatra that he intends to treat her well in Act 5, scene 2
8 Cleopatra, when her first attempt to take her life is foiled in Act 5, scene 2
9 Dercetas, arriving at Caesar's camp with news of Antony's death in Act 5, scene 1
10 Cleopatra, just before she commits suicide in Act 5, Scene 2

Open quotes

1 'That sucks the nurse asleep?' Cleopatra, talking in Act 5, scene 2, to Charmian about the asp she has applied to her breast

2 '... from the monument;/She shall be buried by her Antony.' Caesar, talking to his men at the end of Act 5, scene 2
3 'now from head to foot I am marble-constant: now the fleeting moon/No planet is of mine.' Cleopatra, in a soliloquy in Act 5, scene 2
4 '... which thou/So sought'st to hinder.' Dolabella, talking to the guards as Caesar approaches the dead Cleopatra in Act 5, scene 2
5 '... which kept their course, and lighted/The little O, the earth.' Cleopatra, talking to Dolabella in Act 5, scene 2, about Antony
6 'Cleopatra boy my greatness/I' the posture of a whore.' Cleopatra, talking in Act 5, scene 2, to Iras and Charmian about how she will be treated in Rome
7 'Lest, in her greatness, by some mortal stroke/She do defeat us.' Caesar, talking to Proculeius in Act 5, scene 1, about the precautions which must be taken to ensure that Cleopatra does not take her own life and thereby rob Caesar of the opportunity to display her as a prize in Rome
8 'A lass unparallel'd.' Charmian, in a soliloquy over the dead body of Cleopatra in Act 5, scene 2
9 'Lay me stark-nak'd, and let the water-flies/Blow me into abhorring.' Cleopatra, talking in Act 5, scene 2, to Proculeius about how she would rather die horribly than be taken as a captive prize to Rome
10 '...should make/A greater crack.' Caesar, talking in Act 5, scene 1, to his council of war about the death of Antony

Writing an examination essay

Take the following to heart

- *Carefully study each of the questions set on a particular text* Make sure you understand what they are asking for so that you select the one you know most about.
- *Answer the question* Obvi... isn't it? But bitter experience shows that many students fail because they do not actually answer the question that has been set.
- *Answer all the question* Again, obvious, but so many students spend all their time answering just part of a question and ignoring the rest. This prevents you gaining marks for the parts left out.

The question

1. Read and understand every word of it. If it asks you to compare (the similarities) and/or contrast (the differences) between characters or events, then that is what you must do.
2. Underline all the key words and phrases that mention characters, events and themes, and all instructions as to what to do, e.g. compare, contrast, outline, comment, give an account, write about, show how/what/where.
3. Now write a short list of the things you have to do, one item under the other. A typical question will only have between two and five items at most for you to cope with.

Planning your answer

1. Look at each of the points you have identified from the question. Think about what you are going to say about each. Much of it will be pretty obvious, but if you think of any good ideas, jot them down before you forget them.
2. Decide in what order you are going to deal with the question's major points. Number them in sequence.
3. So far you have done some concentrated, thoughtful reading and written down maybe fifteen to twenty words. You know roughly what you are going to say in response to the question and in what order – if you do not, you have time to give serious thought to trying one of the other questions.

Putting pen to paper

The first sentences are important. Try to summarise your response to the question so the examiner has some idea of how you are going to approach it. Do not say 'I am going to write about the character of Macbeth and show how evil he was' but instead write 'Macbeth was a weak-willed, vicious traitor. Totally dominated by his "fiend-like queen", he deserved the epitaph "this dead butcher" – or did he?' Jump straight into the essay, do not nibble at its extremities for a page and a half. High marks will be gained by the candidate who can show he or she has a mind engaged with the text. Your personal response is rewarded – provided you are answering the question!

As you write your essay *constantly refer back to your list of points* and make sure you are actually responding to them.

How long should it be?

There is no 'correct' length. What you must do is answer the question set, fully and sensitively in the time allowed. Allocate time to each question according to the percentage of marks awarded for it.

How much quotation or paraphrase?

Use only that which is relevant and contributes to the quality and clarity of your answer. Padding is a waste of your time and gains not a single mark.